SSR Paper 17

Rethinking Community Policing in International Police Reform: Examples from Asia

Deniz Kocak

]u[

ubiquity press
London

DCAF

DCAF
Geneva

Published by
Ubiquity Press Ltd.
6 Osborn Street, Unit 2N
London E1 6TD

First published 2018

Cover image: "UNPOL and Timorese Police Officers Visit Dili Orphanage"
Martine Perret © United Nations.
All rights reserved. Image used in this publication under Fair Use permissions.

Printed in the UK by Lightning Source Ltd.
Print and digital versions typeset by Siliconchips Services Ltd.

ISBN (Paperback): 978-1-911529-44-6
ISBN (PDF): 978-1-911529-45-3
ISBN (EPUB): 978-1-911529-46-0
ISBN (Mobi): 978-1-911529-47-7

DOI: https://doi.org/10.5334/bcb

Series: SSR Papers
ISSN (Print) 2571-9289
ISSN (Online) 2571-9297

The full text of this book has been peer-reviewed to ensure high academic standards. For full review policies, see http://www.ubiquitypress.com/

Suggested citation:
Kocak, D. 2018. *Rethinking Community Policing in International Police Reform: Examples from Asia*. London: Ubiquity Press. DOI: https://doi.org/10.5334/bcb. License: CC-BY 4.0

To read the free, open access version of this book online, visit https://doi.org/10.5334/bcb or scan this QR code with your mobile device:

Contents

SSR Papers

The DCAF SSR Papers provide original, innovative and provocative analysis on the challenges of security sector governance and reform. Combining theoretical insight with detailed empirically-driven explorations of state-of-the-art themes, SSR Papers bridge conceptual and pragmatic concerns. Authored, edited and peer reviewed by SSR experts, the series provides a unique platform for in-depth discussion of a governance-driven reform agenda, addressing the overlapping interests of researchers, policy-makers and practitioners in the fields of development, peace and security.

The Geneva Centre for the Democratic Control of Armed Forces (DCAF) is dedicated to making states and people safer. Good security sector governance, based on the rule of law and respect for human rights, is the very basis of development and security. DCAF assists partner states in developing laws, institutions, policies and practices to improve the governance of their security sector through inclusive and participatory reforms based on international norms and good practices.

About the author

Deniz Kocak is currently a Research Associate with the German Federal Institute for Risk Assessment. Prior to this, he worked on and in Timor-Leste with the DFG-Collaborative Research Centre 700 "Governance in Areas of Limited Statehood" and with the United Nations Development Programme (UNDP). He studied history and political science at Humboldt University, the University of Potsdam and Chulalongkorn University, and holds a PhD in political science from the Freie University Berlin.

Declaration

Acknowledgements

The author would like to thank the editor of Ubiquity Press, Fairlie Chappuis and Jasper Linke for their most helpful comments and support, as well as Claudia Jimena Torres and Tim Parsons for conducting a thorough peer review of the paper. The author also acknowledges and thanks Euclides Belo, Nélson de Sousa C. Belo, Beth Greener, Loro Horta, Douglas Kammen, Stephen Kissik, Steffen Lepa, Longuinhos Monteiro, Stephen Moore, Henri Myrttinen, Dominik Nagl, Alberto Quintão de Olivera, Clara Portela, Gordon Peake, Edward Rees, Anacleto da Costa Ribeiro, Ursula C. Schroeder, Leonard C. Sebastian, Cameron Sigley, John G. Taylor, and Todd Wassel for their most helpful support, information or feedback during the research process.

Introduction: Community Policing between Aspiration and Reality

In 2014, United Nations Security Council resolutions on security sector reform (SSR) and on police operations as part of UN missions confirmed the stated aim to seek the sustained implementation of a "community-oriented approach" to policing in the respective mission countries.[1] While promoting the implementation of community-oriented policing since for more than a decade,[2] a clarification of what this approach should actually entail and how exactly the UN missions and operating UN agencies in as diverse country contexts such as Papua-New Guinea, Ukraine, or South-Sudan should pursue this approach is still missing.

Community policing has been increasingly promoted, particularly in liberal democratic societies, as a suitable approach to improve police service and effectiveness along the lines of democratic governance, to reduce the fear of crime within the communities and to overcome mutual distrust between the police and the communities by enhancing police-citizen partnerships. This, advertised as a best-practice approach to policing, soon found its way into the evolving international state-building and development agenda and became part of various development catalogues. In most cases, international donors tried to implement community policing in developing and transitional countries through short-term workshops and best-practice training manuals modelled on community-oriented policing approaches in liberal democratic societies. While these training programmes were probably designed with the best of intentions, they not only lacked relevance to the actual socio-political realities and challenges in most of the countries where the police reform programmes were initiated. The majority of the programmes also lacked a sound and congruent understanding of what community policing should actually be. Given the myriad of patchy definitional understandings and interpretations of and approaches to community policing in various countries, it is not surprising that internationally driven police reform initiatives aiming at the establishment of community policing in developing and transitional countries resulted in fair outcomes at best.[3]

Whereas most of the existing literature on international police reform endeavours puts its focus on technical and financial capacities only, so far there is a shortage of research that deals with the

How to cite this book chapter:
Kocak, D. 2018. *Rethinking Community Policing in International Police Reform: Examples from Asia.* Pp. 1–2. London: Ubiquity Press. DOI: https://doi.org/10.5334/bcb.a. License: CC-BY 4.0

actual impact of historical trajectories, cultures, and patterns of policing on contemporary SSR endeavours in the context of developing and transitional countries. Additionally, the concept of community policing remains particularly inconclusive and is still subject to various interpretations without the actual critical contextualization of its historical origins.

The merit of historically informed analysis of contemporary policies and political challenges is undisputed.[4] However, only a few publications regarding security and developmental policy actually problematize historical legacies and their impact on contemporary security challenges, as, among others, Egnell and Haldén argue.[5] Due to the dearth of historical inquiry in international security studies, the paper explicitly applies a historical perspective to investigate the origins and transformations of community-oriented policing.

By recapitulating existing ambiguities, disarray and confusion on the concept of community policing, its frequent but uncritical equation with democratic policing, and its simultaneous advertisement as a best-practice measure for police reform in developing and transitional countries, several questions arise: (1) What are the actual historical origins of present-day community policing, (2) what are the necessary conditions to establish community policing, and (3) to what extent is it possible to promote and to establish community policing along the lines of good governance and SSR in developing and transitional countries?

To answer these research questions, the paper critically examines the historical origins of community policing and, in addition to it, draws on a conceptual framework of adaptation processes in governance transfers. Moreover, the paper makes a clear distinction between means and ends in community policing in order to highlight important technical and practical similarities but differences in political country contexts and normative objectives of police reform.

It has to be stressed that normative objectives of police reform in non-democratic political systems differ substantially from democratic political systems. Depending on the actual political agenda, non-democratic political systems may particularly focus on surveillance and social-control elements of community policing that foster security. In contrast, democratic political systems generally follow the aim of implementing a variant of community policing that ideally fosters a service-oriented, accountable and people-centred security environment by the police, an approach that has been theoretically underpinned by John Alderson[6] and Herman Goldstein,[7] among others.

By utilising the devised conceptual framework on adaptation processes, the discussed cases of Victorian Britain, Imperial and post-war Japan, Singapore, and Timor-Leste reveal important preconditions, dynamics, and setbacks regarding prospects and limitations of implementing community-oriented approaches to policing. In essence, the paper argues that the historical origins of community policing were not directed at improving police-community relations in the first place, but at more effective surveillance and control mechanisms to uphold state security instead. Whereas contemporary approaches to community-oriented policing in line with SSR and good governance are tightly connected to political pluralist and liberal democratic norms and values, the basic concept of community policing itself is not bound to pluralist political systems.

Furthermore, it is argued that basic bureaucratic police professionalism and capacities are necessary conditions to establish community policing as part of SSR endeavours in the context of developing or transitional countries. Moreover, the actual political will and commitment of local authorities to push for reforms is required to establish a viable and sustained local approach to community-oriented policing. Finally, external reform programmes need to be adjusted to the respective country context. This requires international donors not only to manage their expectations on a frictionless implementation phase but also to be more flexible in their approaches to reform.

International Police Reform Initiatives in the Context of SSR

The concept of SSR gained prominence during the 1990s within the thematic areas of development and policy as well as within academia. The most frequently cited definition of SSR is the rather broad approach by the OECD-Development Assistance Committee,[8] which includes, apart from the traditional security actors and established political institutions, also non-state actors as central actors in SSR. According to the OECD-DAC, SSR comprises the establishment of sustained, transparent, and accountable rule of law-based and legitimate and civilian-led national security governance that is guided along democratic norms and principles.[9] Meanwhile, the UN's definition of SSR[10] holds to lead the way by stressing the indispensable importance of national ownership, the necessary support for national reform efforts by international actors, and a comprehensive approach to reform, both in technical as well as political terms.

The concept, originally based on traditional security and development studies as well as civil-military relations, soon evolved into an important framework for reform initiatives within the security sectors of developing countries as part of the overall *liberal peace* and *good governance* paradigm.[11] Externally driven and implemented SSR measures therefore included comprehensive institutional reform and restructuring programmes of national security sector governance architectures in transitional and developing countries. These measures particularly aimed at the establishment of legitimate civilian control of the national security sector and a professionalization of the national security actors in line with the SSR agenda. Hence, an important step in course of the reform process is the establishment of an oversight function on behalf of legitimate civilian representatives over the main relevant security sector institutions and organizations. These are, in general, the line ministries of the interior, justice, defence, foreign affairs, and finance as well as corresponding committees. Moreover, independent oversight bodies such as the ombuds-institution or national non-governmental organizations, human rights groups, and research institutions can play a decisive role in oversight management.[12]

How to cite this book chapter:

Kocak, D. 2018. *Rethinking Community Policing in International Police Reform: Examples from Asia.* Pp. 3–9. London: Ubiquity Press. DOI: https://doi.org/10.5334/bcb.b. License: CC-BY 4.0

While reform initiatives are ideally triggered through the relevant ministries, reforms do also aim explicitly at the main executive institutions such as the national police, the national military as well as the national intelligence agencies and affiliated institutions. Main reform initiatives comprise the revision of national doctrines, laws, and decrees that are relevant to the security sector and the overall political constitution. Moreover, internal control mechanisms within each relevant executive institution aim at more transparent and accountable self-control of the respective security actors to ensure rule of law-based and human rights oriented courses of action.[13] Apart from overall institutional reform initiatives, comprehensive training and support of local members of parliament as well as of ministry officials is essential to ensure necessary professional expertise on matters of security governance, a topic that is in many developing and transitional countries still a domain of security actors and their associates only.[14]

Capacity building as part of SSR endeavours is vital to ensure a sustained and continued transformation of the security sector. Capacity building measures, however, should not be simply equated with train-and-equip programmes, a strategy often used by the USSR or the USA during the Cold War to ensure military capabilities on behalf of their respective proxies in developing countries.[15] Moreover, technical and operational capacity building needs to be embedded into an overarching reform program that ensures an interlink between normative institutional reform along the lines of SSR principles and technical or operational abilities of the local security forces. Neglecting institutional reform while delivering operational training only will admittedly lead to a more effective security actor in terms of improved tactical abilities but may also result, in the worst case, in increased abuse of power.[16]

Rather, capacity building measures, particularly for national police forces, are an important tool not only to establish a functioning police who are able to perform day-to-day policing tasks but also to ensure that the objectives of democratic governance are actually implemented and followed within the organizational apparatus. Training in human resources management, for instance, helps to professionalize the bureaucratic capabilities by establishing databases and archives on officer's personnel files, and expedites overall organizational development. Capacity building in this area enables the HR section and the police command to facilitate performance reviews on a regular basis, to file entries on complaints or misconduct of police officers, and therefore leads, ideally, to improved oversight, and to a more disciplined and law-abiding police corps. As for another area, assets management and procurement are relevant to monitor the police budget and to prevent instances of misappropriation, excessive spending, or corruption. Hence, a professional asset-management unit will contribute to increased accountability and transparency of police spending. Moreover, professional asset management ensures that the procurement policies are in line with the police's annual action plans and the general strategic planning.[17] In short, capacity building is an important part of democratic governance programming due to the fact that it supports the police's institutional functioning and facilitates the implementation of SSR inherent norms and values.[18]

Finally, since SSR is more than technical support but aims at one of the most sensitive and contested domains of national sovereignty, the state's monopoly on the use of force and the control over the national security actors, SSR is without doubt a political task. Moreover, the SSR agenda is clearly motivated along Western liberal norms and values as well as along democratic principles of policy making.[19] Therefore, implementing SSR constitutes a veritable challenge to SSR programmers and practitioners since the local realities and political conditions in a given mission country might contradict the very foundations of SSR inherent norms of democratic governance and principles of human rights. And undeniably, SSR may be a tightrope walk for local reformers and external practitioners alike due to the challenge of harmonizing normative and ethical guidelines of SSR with the realities, and often confined spaces for action, in the respective countries.

SSR Initiatives and Local Ownership

As empirical evidence suggests after almost two decades of SSR, sustained implementation of intended SSR initiatives in developing and transitional countries requires first and foremost the genuine support of the national political leadership,[20] a fact which has been recently reiterated by the United Nations Security Council Resolutions on SSR and on international police units as part of UN missions.[21]

The existence of local ownership, the actual political will and aspiration on behalf of the local political leadership to support and to advance initiated reform attempts, is essential to success and sustained political change.[22] This means in practical terms that local actors have a determining influence on the outline, programming, implementation, and evaluation of reform activities in their respective countries.[23] While the idea of local ownership sounds convincing in theory, the actual realization of local ownership faced several difficulties on behalf of the external and the local actors alike. In fact, several cases of SSR unveiled the problem that the local political elite was not able to assert itself against external SSR programmers, either due to internal rivalries or due to a lack of profound political and technical expertise. Hence, reform initiatives were implemented by external actors without the actual support and substantial input of local decision makers. As a consequence, resistance or negligence on behalf of the local political leadership against the perceived "imposed" reform programmes followed soon.[24]

Then there is also the question of who the most suited local counterpart actually is. For a reason, Lee and Özerdem[25] point out that "the locals" are not a collective or uniform actor but consist out of myriad individuals driven by diverging political interests. Still there is an inconclusive debate about identifying local partners by external programmers to cooperate with. While the local political elite seems to be the most appropriate and convenient counterpart in addressing questions of security sector-related reforms, there are also arguments about the necessity to include local non-governmental organizations and civil-society organizations to cover a broader political spectrum. In essence, approaching the local government that is generally interested in maintaining the political status quo will not necessarily bring the anticipated will for change.[26]

Moreover, there are also empirical cases where there is a strong local ownership driven by their own ideas about the purpose and direction of SSR initiatives. As the study of police reform in Bosnia-Herzegovina by Muehlmann[27] indicates, local partners do not always share the fundamental values and norms of good security governance, but rather make use of foreign-trained and foreign-supported local police forces for personal and financial interests.[28] Even addressing local NGOs, CSOs, or customary elites to forestall potential misuse of funds and resources by established local political elites might not bring the aimed-for reliable partner in SSR initiatives. Rather, complex local political rivalries and grievances could not only inhibit SSR programming but also lead to renewed hostilities. Moreover, local political elites as well as NGOs or customary elites could pursue reforms that run counter to the donor's expectations of good governance and human rights.[29] Therefore, Albrecht[30] correctly notes that local ownership of externally initiated reforms only occurs if the local decision makers do not perceive the reform initiatives as a threat towards their long-term political and personal interests and if they agree with the reform agenda.

The Centrality of Police Reform in SSR

In daily interactions with the community, the police are the most visible representation of the government. The police are therefore the ultimate interface between a country's citizens and government. In this position, the police not only carry out the executive mandate but also act as mediator between different social groups and political factions. In short, the performance of the police is ultimately a display of the state's political and social agenda. Since the police are such an important domestic actor in terms of security provision, social mediation, and ideally, being a role model for the population regarding the protection of civic norms and values, reforming the police along the principles of good governance is a major aim of international police reform initiatives in developing and transitional countries.[31]

International peacekeeping missions with considerable contingents of police units under the guidance of the United Nations increased dramatically since the end of the Cold War. The conflict scenarios of the 1990s reflected a changing geopolitical environment and, as a consequence, a different kind of conflict. Henceforward, the UN peacekeeping unit's tasks were not the monitoring of ceasefires between warring states and national militaries anymore, but containing civil wars and large-scale internal conflicts between warring alliances of warlords, militias, and governmental forces in fragile states.[32] These "new wars"[33] often resulted in a partial or even complete breakdown of state structures and governance provisions, such as the collapse of the local security sector. Realizing the changed geopolitical challenges, the international community reformulated its overall programmatic commitment through Boutros-Ghali's "Agenda for Peace" as well as the Brahimi report on how to respond to these kinds of conflicts.[34]

Since then, international police units, alongside the established "blue helmet" forces and under the guidance of the United Nations, were deployed to fill the security vacuum in a given country and tasked with rebuilding basic security structures in line with the international liberal peace and good governance agenda.[35] In contrast to the traditional deployment of "blue helmet" military units, the deployment of international police components facilitated an overall diversification of the mission's operation strategies, made them more flexible, and, as Call and Barnett[36] put it, created a "second generation of peacekeeping". Hence, the police are ideally trained for communication and day-to-day interaction with the local population; a skill set which regular military units usually do not possess.[37] This close contact on a daily basis between the multinational police and the local population would enable the United Nations police officers to promote the pluralist and liberal democratic values in the host country, ideally.[38]

However, these new deployments and tasks for multinational police contingents brought institutional as well as programmatic challenges and shortcomings to light: Being responsible for security provision, training, and mentoring the local police forces, United Nations Police contingents soon became overstretched in regards to technical expertise and the ability to actually train their local counterparts. Most important, however, a defined understanding of what kind of approach to policing should actually be implemented by the United Nations Police was missing. Official guidelines for multinational police units as part of UN peacekeeping missions were not established before 2000.[39] The then-formulated "democratic policing" – or interchangeably used "community-oriented policing" as an envisaged policing approach in the respective mission countries[40] – proved to be a rather vaguely defined ideal conception than an applicable model for police reform in fragile environments.[41] While the importance of the international police units as part of the United Nations missions has been recently substantiated by the United Nations Security Council Resolutions 2151 and 2185 in 2014,[42] and a community-oriented approach to policing has been reiterated as the envisaged policing approach, an actual definition of what this community-oriented approach actually entails is still missing.

Rethinking "Democratic Policing"

Assuming that there is a basic model of policing in contemporary democracies which ultimately rests on the Peelian metropolitan policing,[43] Bayley, among others, presented an ideal type of policing in democratic societies. Contrary to existing debates about pros and cons of centralised or decentralised organisational police models and their respective ability or inability to allow effective and democratically oriented policing, Bayley highlights the actual implementation of policing on the ground and the daily interactions of police officers with the citizens as a possible indicator to measure democratic policing. There are four cornerstones of democratic policing: To act in accordance with the rule of law, to respect the universal human rights, to adhere to transparency and accountability, and to understand policing as a service of the police towards its citizens.[44]

Policing according to the rule of law prevents arbitrary actions of police officers and simultaneously ensures that the police act according to fixed principles of law.[45] Rule of law by itself, however, does not guarantee the protection of citizens from police abuse of power, as Call and Bayley argue.[46] Therefore, not only rule of law principles should guide the police's behaviour but also principles of fundamental human rights. Furthermore, *transparency and accountability* of the police towards the political leadership and the respective population are necessary to strengthen trust of the population in the police force as well as to enable a comprehensive legitimate civilian control over the national police.[47] Finally, it is important that the national police are an inherent part of the state and act accordingly as a partner and service agency for the collective good of the people and public security. To achieve this end, the police should approach the public through various channels of communication and thereby generate public trust.[48]

The idea of a universal democratic policing model, however, faced resistance from several scholars since the devised term "democratic policing" might appear as just another label for already established policing practices and, furthermore, bears with the politically charged term "democratic" a clear normative and exclusive connotation.[49] In this vein, Sklansky[50] also points to the fact that the definition of "democracy" has a huge range and is also subject to a specific generational and historical understanding.

Similarly, there are conceptual misunderstandings in the common assumption which unconditionally links democratic policing to community policing[51] such as the OSCE does in its "Guidebook on Democratic Policing".[52] Community policing indisputably entails theoretical origins and many elements similar to democratic policing. However, for that reason alone, community policing is still ambiguously and inconclusively defined, a problem that even the OSCE admits.[53] Moreover, the interrelated fact that community policing techniques are also utilized by authoritarian governments to establish comprehensive surveillance and control of their citizens for the sake of state security should provide ample food for thought.[54]

However, the proposed theorizing on "core policing" by Bayley and Perito[55] might strike a middle course to the normatively charged terminology of "democratic policing" and "community policing". The authors argue that core policing constitutes first and foremost a certain state of mind as to a service-oriented and impartial police organization. This service orientation of the police manifests itself in three overarching guidelines: "being available", "being helpful", and "being fair and respectful".[56] Displaying approachability and the willingness to take security concerns of the citizens seriously is essential to gain trust and confidence within the communities. Helpfulness of the police towards the communities, even in stressful situations, fosters the peoples' belief in the ethical and rule-based working attitude of the police officers. Finally, fairness and respectful interaction of the police, regardless of social standing, ethnicity, or gender, with the communities displays a service attitude towards the greater common good of a society. Unsurprisingly, Bayley and Perito refer to the similarities between core policing and community policing. However, they also stress the necessity of establishing the police officers' mindset according to the principles of core policing first before aiming at more complex ideational concepts such as community policing.[57]

While the service orientation towards society on behalf of the police and police impartiality are basic requirements for plural policing, necessary development of police capabilities, standard operational procedures, and police management would help to complement the overall professional police development in transitional and post-conflict countries.

A Conceptual Framework on Adaptation Processes in Police Reform Scenarios

Referring back to existing research on governance transfers, exchanges – both of an ideational or material kind – between different cultures are a common pattern of transnational and global interaction whereby transfers were not only unidirectional from north to south but multidirectional.[58] One of many examples for multidirectional influences is, for instance, the Royal Irish Constabulary (RIC), which has been adjusted according to the policing experiences in the British colonies.[59] Martin Thomas describes the general colonial policing approach as a "hybrid" blend consisting of metropolitan, colonial, as well as customary forms of local policing.[60] In fact, adaptation processes, as Rinke et al.[61] argue, were born out of necessity to actually implement external concepts and norms in colonial settings. Without the ability to adjust to the respective context, external actors would have not been able to assert their rule at all.

Before approaching present day challenges to police reform on a theoretical level and reflecting about adaptation and resistance processes, though, it makes sense to consider Crewe's[62] findings on adaption, conflict, and resistance: First, there is much more than plain success or apparent failure in interaction processes between groups or individuals. Second, resistance or noncompliance are not necessarily displayed in violent behaviour or open hostilities but may also come in disguise. Third, Crewe cautions that the absence of open rebellion or resistance does not necessarily mean that an introduced system is actually supported or even accepted by the receiving side.[63]

Several authors writing on police reform in transitional or post-conflict countries applied the terms "adaptation" and "resistance" to describe difficulties between external and local actors during the actual reform processes.[64] Uildriks and van Reenen, for instance, argue that the local police in their discussed case study had the choice to either resist externally proposed reform programs or to adapt to them in order to have an impact on the future policing approach.[65] While these descriptive accounts on adaptation and resistance processes in police reform scenarios make a lot of sense, it appears necessary to make use of a theory-led conceptual framework.[66] Inductive reasoning and theory building will expand our knowledge on interactions between external and local actors in the course of police reform initiatives and might even answer to the still-inconclusive debate on local ownership.

The transfer and adaptation process initially starts when an unfamiliar concept is presented by external actors to local actors. This is followed by an adaptation process executed through a local and/or an external agency. It is important to note that the adaptation process means that the erstwhile unfamiliar concept passes a process of transformation. This adjustment to the local context and environment is necessary to establish points of intersection between external and local paradigms of thought and action. Without the adaptation process to the local context, the concept would remain meaningless to the local actors and would be therefore neglected. But contrary to earlier accounts on transfer processes, the willingness of the receivers to adapt is not necessarily bound to material incentives only. Rather, the prospect of expanding technical knowledge and courses of action are in many cases motivation enough to incorporate new concepts into their own repertoire.[67] The adaptation process of the new concept on behalf of the local actors alters its content and scope, without a doubt. This however, is a necessary step during the adaptation process which enables the respective actors to reinterpret the concept along local paradigms of thought and action. This adaptation process to the local context particularly enables the involved actors to apply an otherwise inapplicable concept.[68]

The developed conceptual framework will not only help to answer the initial research questions, but will also enable us to analyse, reflect, and understand transfers of policing paradigms across national and cultural boundaries. Using the lens of adaptation, resistance, and reinterpretation with regard to police reform in past and present scenarios will yield new insights of when and how SSR and good governance initiatives might eventually thrive.

Methodologically, the paper draws on a small-N design, and the case selection for chapter three and four of the paper rests on a nominal and focussed comparison. Following the logic of J.S. Mill's causal inference and method of agreement, the paper's cross-case analysis enables us to compare and to contrast selected cases in order to learn about necessary causes and conditions for community policing.[69] Therefore, cases of Imperial and post-war Japan, Singapore, and Timor-Leste are deliberately chosen to contrast, illustrate, and exemplify results of police reform and, in particular, the local implementation strategies of various strands of community policing.

It becomes clear, that the independent variable "local ownership", or rather, "the existence of local ownership" is crucial for the implementation process, which is hereafter operationalized as dependent variable ("adaptation" or "reinterpretation"), of different philosophical and technical variants of community policing in the treated cases, whereas other potentially significant variables, such as the political system in the respective country or the respective historical timeframe in which the transfer took place, can be ruled out.

The paper is based on secondary literature, policy reports, legislative texts, and resolutions. Furthermore, insights from qualitative semi-structured interviews with police officers, international police advisers, UN officials, and representatives of NGOs serve as additional sources for the empirical case studies. The interviews were conducted between 2011 and 2015, and the identity of the interview partners has been, by request, anonymized.

The paper is structured as follows: The second chapter presents and discusses contemporary approaches to and varieties of community policing. The third chapter traces the frequently cited but often neglected historical origins of community policing – the 19th century British *metropolitan policing* and the *koban* policing of Imperial and post-war Japan. This is followed by the fourth chapter, which deals with international transfers of community policing in the recent past and discusses the implementation of community-oriented approaches to policing in Singapore and in Timor-Leste. Chapter five finally discusses the case studies' main findings, provides answers to the initial research questions, and concludes with several recommendations.

Situating Community Policing in Contemporary Approaches to Public Order

As a consequence of deteriorated police-citizen relations in the course of the peace movement and mass demonstrations against police brutality as well as against continued discriminatory practices of police officers against members of ethnic minorities during the 1970s, police commissioners and politicians were, as Bayley and Shearing put it, "desperately searching for new approaches".[70]

The main idea of community policing rests on the attempt to leave behind purely reactive and traditional approaches to policing. Since a reactive approach to policing is, according to Alderson, not conducive to policing in a democratic political system due to the fact that it creates a particular distance between the police and the citizens since a contact and communicative exchange takes place only in cases of emergency, a proactive form of policing and a fundamental and trustful cooperation between the police and the population is intended to establish public security and societal peace. Furthermore, a community-oriented and proactive approach to policing would find appropriate and well-suited means to protect the respective residents according to their needs.[71]

Through active and continued communication with the local residents, so the argument goes, the police would be able to identify the most pressing problems of the respective neighbourhood and try to cooperatively find workable and sustained solutions. The established reactive approach to policing relied heavily on patrol cars, and therefore led to a social alienation between the police and the communities since the police became unapproachable by the public. By contrast, proponents of community policing highlighted the importance of foot patrols by police officers to show police presence on the streets and to enable the residents to approach the police officers with their concerns. Foot patrols therefore appeared as a feasible technique to regain the trust of the residents in the police and to simultaneously enable police officers to learn about the residents

How to cite this book chapter:
Kocak, D. 2018. *Rethinking Community Policing in International Police Reform: Examples from Asia.* Pp. 11–16. London: Ubiquity Press. DOI: https://doi.org/10.5334/bcb.c. License: CC-BY 4.0

living in their assigned working districts. These confidence-building measures of the police are particularly targeted at ethnic minorities since these members of society have suffered the most from police brutality and discriminatory practices by the police in the past.[72]

The idea of implementing a more community-oriented approach to policing in the UK was a reaction to the shattered relations between the police and communities during the 1970s. As opposed to the existing reactive approach to policing in the UK, Alderson reasoned about improving police-community relations through a proactive service attitude of the police toward the communities. Hence, he outlined principles for an aspired approach to rule-based and indiscriminate policing: "To contribute towards liberty, equality and fraternity in human affairs; to help reconcile freedom with security and to uphold the rule of law; to facilitate the achievement of human dignity through upholding and protecting human rights and the pursuit of happiness; to contribute towards the creation of reinforcement of trust in communities; to strengthen the security and the feeling of security of persons and property; and to investigate, detect and activate the prosecution of offences within the rule of law."[73] Policing, as Alderson continues, is essential to safeguarding the people's freedom, physical security, and to protecting them from fear.[74] It should be noted that the essence of Alderson's envisaged policing principles corresponds with the concept of human security as well as the conviction that policing in a liberal-democratic society is a common good.[75]

The notion of a necessary realignment of policing in liberal-democratic societies was reiterated by the Scarman Report of 1981.[76] The Scarman Report was based on an investigation on the causes of the so-called Brixton Riots. The report's main findings revolved around the need to readjust the British police's robust and discriminatory policing and to transform it towards a more service-oriented approach to policing, particularly towards ethnic minorities in socially deprived areas. Lord Scarman identified particularly the disturbed community-police relations as a barrier to prevent outbursts of violence such as the Brixton Riots, and therefore highlighted the importance of consensual cooperation between the communities and the police and increased lines of communication.[77]

Hence, as a reaction to the Brixton Riots and the concomitant Scarman Report, approaches to community-oriented policing by Alderson[78] and the "multi-agency approach" by Newman[79] became a viable alternative to the heretofore predominant reactive policing in the UK.[80] Aiming at increased police-community consultation to prevent and fight crime, the approach of proactive community-oriented and multi-agency policing also deemed to improve shattered police-community relations in the long run.[81] Since then, community policing has been increasingly publicized and advertised in the United States of America and other Western countries as the most suitable approach to strengthening the communities' trust into the police and to promote police-citizen partnerships.

Community policing was soon labelled by police officials and politicians as the "sole alternative"[82] not only to overcome the loss of trust of the people into the police and to reconcile the problematic police-citizen relations in an ethnic heterogeneous and politically pluralist country, but also to decrease the high incidence of crime in the United States. The increasing popularity of community policing, however, diluted its actual theoretical and normative substance. Original forms of community policing were traced back by community policing proponents to the *metropolitan policing*, introduced by Sir Robert Peel in Britain in the 19th century and to the Japanese *koban* policing. Both, the metropolitan policing as well as the *koban* policing were deemed to be based on a *close* and *trustful* relationship between the police and the population.

Since the 1990s, the majority of the communal police stations in the United States officially introduced community policing into their work.[83] Moreover, this advertised new approach to policing allowed police commissioners and academics to receive research funds or support money for facilitating community policing through expert assessments or the visible implementation of community policing elements into the actual police service, as Carter and Manning state.[84] In fact, as part of the emerging trend to publicly advertise community policing as the most suitable tool to overcome the distorted relations between the police and ethnic minorities, and to decrease the high crime rates in many American cities, a great number of police commissioners established community policing programmes and special units responsible for community policing in the respective municipalities. According to Mastrofski[85], having necessary electoral support in mind during the coming elections, these publicly advertised innovations should give the impression that the respective political administration and police leadership is open to new approaches and amicable police-community relations.

Establishing special police units and departments for the purpose of conducting community policing within the respective municipalities, however, appears to be unrewarding. Community policing is not only a technique but also a specific philosophy and mindset of how to approach underlying causes for social conflict, violence, and poverty, of how to treat and how to police the population in line with the principles of fundamental human rights, non-discriminatory behaviour towards ethnic, religious, and sexual diversity, and a sound understanding of the rule of law. Therefore, ideally this particular mindset of community policing needs to be guiding the actions of every police officer in the respective police station to trigger a change of police behaviour and practices. However, insulating community policing in special police units or departments runs counter to the actual idea of reforming the police according to principles of community policing. Moreover, following different approaches of policing within a single police station, as some observers caution,[86] may lead to parallel policing realities for the police officers and, at worst, to conflicts and rivalries about the "real" approach to policing. Still, police work is generally perceived as acting in suspense-packed and physically challenging situations and is frequently linked to ideas about transfigured masculinity. While popular narratives on the police culture hold that "true" police work would enable male police officers to prove their virility, administrative activities and "softer" forms of police work such as communication-based engagement with the public is often described as boring and linked to "effeminate" attributes and behaviour.[87]

Community policing is not limited to close contacts between the police and residents only, such as approachable police officers walking the beat, house visits, or police-community meetings. Rather, following a community-oriented approach of policing means a thorough reform and transformation of the police and the way they perceive and protect the community.

Since community policing sets its focus on proactive engagement with the public and there-fore entails the ability of the police officer to mediate and communicate reasonably with her or his respective counterpart, this "soft policing" approach faces resistance from police officers as well. Particularly the strand of research on police culture[88] mainly argues that police practices and the behaviour of police officers towards citizens do not solely follow formal guidelines but are also influenced by informally passed-on experiences, attitudes, and mindsets among the peer group of police officers.[89] Due to the fact that these very informal rules of action do have a major effect on police officers' behaviour towards citizens, the setup of community policing units alone is futile. Rather, implementing community policing starts first and foremost with a mindset change of the police officers and their idea of policing, encompassing all echelons of the institution.[90] In theory, this should be followed by altered operation schedules and strategies, a decentralized police structure, and enhanced discretionary powers for the police officers on the beat.

Voiced criticism on the community policing approach within the police revolves mainly around the perceived non-applicability of purely communication-based policing techniques in the daily life of police officers on the street.[91] Others claim that these "soft" approaches to policing are unrewarding and would not be equivalent to actual police work.[92] Finally, a main reason for resistance against community policing techniques is the outspoken scepticism on behalf of many police officers towards policing concepts and approaches that stem from the desks of police bureaucrats, politicians, and academics.[93]

While the concept of community policing is generally supported within academia, it is rather the misuse and the definitional ambiguity of the community policing concept which encouraged several authors[94] in their criticism on the excessive increase of domestic and international calls for police reform along the lines of community policing. Lyons[95], for instance, conducted research on police-citizen partnerships in Seattle. His main findings suggest that in many cases of police-citizen cooperation schemes, information sharing flows rarely bi-directional but rather unidirectional, from the citizens to the police, indeed, revealing a relatively passive community policing engagement on behalf of the police. Moreover, the increasing ethnic, social, and religious heterogeneity of American urban areas complicates the identification of a common threat perception and articulation. This, of course, raises the question of who the actual "citizen counterpart" for the police is. According to Lyons,[96] the police in Seattle identified the local chamber of commerce as the sole citizen counterpart while neglecting to include several well-organized local civil society organizations. The police-citizen cooperation was therefore limited to a selected, small, exclusive, and rather wealthy segment of Seattle's population.

Consequences of these practices of unilaterally chosen partners might lead to a prioritization of security needs and expectations for a small, potentially rather homogeneous, and wealthier part of the society. Simultaneously, deprived areas with rather higher crime rates might easily get into the focus of hot-spot policing. Hence, policing along ethnic profiling or style of clothing are determining whether one would get into the focus of police measures or not. While these very residential areas particularly might need communication-based and community-oriented policing strategies the most, heavy-handed policing strategies conducted by police task forces impede police-citizen communication on equal footing.[97] Moreover, as Dixon[98] argues, if one would understand community policing as a policing approach that tackles the most acute security threats in a respective community, each and any policing strategy, from preventive "soft policing" to reactive or militarized policing could be designated as community policing.

Kraska[99] especially criticises the militarisation of the police in the United States under the pretext of the "community policing" label: Regular raids by heavily armed SWAT units as well as patrols in armoured vehicles with random stop-and-frisk searches of residents in branded hot-spot areas are far more easy to justify to the public if these very measures are connected to a designated community-safety programme. Instead of trying to be approachable to the residents in need, the highly armed appearance of the police rather disturbs police-community relations even more, as he argues.

Varieties of Community Policing

Several approaches to policing have been associated with community-oriented policing so far. Broken-windows policing, zero-tolerance policing, and problem-oriented policing are, among others, regarded as varieties of community-oriented policing strategies. While all listed styles of policing generally engage with the community, there are still differences regarding their normative and disciplinary approaches regarding the community as well as to what extent the communities are actually involved in the provision of security.

Broken-windows policing spread across the United States during the 1980s and has been mainly inspired by a seminal article by Wilson and Kelling[100] on strategies of how to overcome diffuse fear of crime. The authors refer to the metaphor of a broken window to explain the increasing urban dilapidation in combination with rising criminality and insecurity. Wilson and Kelling hypothesize that if a windowpane is broken and no one repairs it soon, remaining windows of the same building will be broken as well since the apparent lack of maintenance might lead to the conclusion that breaking windows of that building will have no consequences for the respective perpetrators at all. Moreover, if, as the argument of Wilson and Kelling continues, the absence of consequences and an associated lawlessness remain for these kinds of delinquencies, defiance of the law will increase and spill over to the whole neighbourhood. As a reaction, the authors conclude, average citizens will increasingly generate diffuse fear of crime on the streets and move away to safer places in the city. The neighbourhood in question, however, will sooner or later be lost.[101]

Using the example of Newark, New Jersey, in the United States, Wilson and Kelling[102] suggest that the reintroduction of foot patrols by the police admittedly did not lead to a decrease of crime in the respective city districts. However, their research indicated that residents generated an increased feeling of security and felt more encouraged to intervene in cases of vandalism or petty crime, having in mind those police officers walking the beat. What is more, the regularly conducted beat patrols enabled the police officers to get to know the respective city district, its residents, and potential troublemakers. Simultaneously, on behalf of the residents there appeared to be a growing awareness that criminal activity and vandalism would immediately be pursued and punished by the police officers in place. In conclusion, the authors argue that the introduction of patrol cars had the effect that police officers became inaccessible to the residents. However, sustained police presence through foot patrol in the city districts would foster better police-citizen relationships and an increased feeling of security on behalf of the residents.[103]

The broken-windows thesis that vandalism and disorder leads to an increase of crime has been disputed within the research community. Moreover, it has been objected that particularly ethnic minorities would disproportionally and unjustifiably become labelled as "troublemakers" and therefore targeted by police officers while following the broken-windows approach.[104] Moreover, adolescents, members of ethnic minorities, or homeless persons could become criminalized by spending time in areas designated for public use since loitering might be perceived as disorderly behaviour. Hence, implementing the broken-windows approach might lead to an immense loss of trust into the actual objectivity and impartiality of the police on behalf of the affected citizens. While the broken-windows approach seems plausible in theory, implementing it would require a highly professional and impartial police force. Otherwise, the proactive character of broken-windows policing could turn quite quickly into repressive policing similar to the zero-tolerance approach.[105]

This zero-tolerance policing is subsumed by Burke[106] as a proactive and assertive policing concept, having its theoretical underpinnings in the broken-windows approach. In contrast to the broken-windows thesis of Wilson and Kelling, however, zero-tolerance policing aims not only to reduce the diffuse feeling of insecurity on behalf of the residents, but also to reduce criminality in the long run. Within criminological theory, policing in New York City is widely regarded as paramount example for zero-tolerance policing when the then-mayor Giuliani heralded the start of a rigorous prosecution of any kind of crime to contain the exuberant crime rates in the metropolis during the late 1990s.[107] Hard-line policing of any petty offense aimed therefore at calling a halt to a normalization of existing law violation in everyday life and at bringing criminals to justice. One of the main objectives of zero-tolerance policing was also to discourage any potential copycat from engaging in criminal activities.[108] Similar to the community policing narrative, zero-tolerance policing proponents claim that this policing approach is backed up by the majority of residents and covers the very security needs of its respective community. In fact, the rigorous policing against any form of crime according to the zero-tolerance approach enjoyed popularity and was received favourably in wide areas of New York City.

However, Lum,[109] among others, cautions that zero-tolerance policing might also lead to a normalization of inappropriate behaviour by police officers, such as harsh treatment of citizens, which might often be disproportional to the respective offence. This behaviour of police officers towards citizens might not be desirable in a political pluralist country. And while Knights[110] admits that zero-tolerance policing might have public appeal by reducing crime rates, he doubts the long-term effectiveness of this approach. Tackling underlying social causes for criminal behaviour and establishing sustained lines of communication between the police and residents will not be achieved through hard-line policing alone, as he argues. Rather, zero-tolerance policing might sooner or later lead to cleavages along social and ethnic lines of society. Again, as Taylor[111] concurs, zero-tolerance policing will, at the end of the day, benefit the wealthier parts of society, while ethnic minorities, adolescents, and the socially weaker parts of society get into the focus of policing measures.

In contrast to the broken-windows approach and zero-tolerance policing, problem-oriented policing (POP) rests on problem-centred analysis, the investigation, and eventually, the settling of causes related to criminality. Goldstein[112] is regarded as one of the forward thinkers of this approach to policing. Criticizing the established reactionary patterns of policing by stating that they do not match the realities of contemporary democratic heterogeneous societies, Goldstein recommended combining the established tools of policing with active and sustained police-citizen cooperation.[113] The main tools for investigation and analysis of POP are the SARA-approach (Scanning, Analysis, Response, Assessment), and data-backed triangulation.[114] With the help of this methodology, the police are able to generate criminal patterns and to accumulate "hot spots" of criminality in urban areas. Additionally, established and trustful lines of communication with the respective residents of a community are necessary to jointly address causes of social instability.

Depending on the respective investigation, different police strategies are devised to cope with the crime in question, ranging from preventive engagement of community-oriented policing to repressive hard-line policing.[115] Braga and Weisburd,[116] for instance, specify "enforcement problem-oriented policing" and "situational problem-oriented policing". While the former approach includes targeted raids, increased car patrols in hot-spot areas, and random body searches of suspected individuals, situational problem-oriented policing includes rather "soft" police measures such as public outreach, increased communication with local civil-society organisations, and an increased harmonization of crime-prevention strategies with other relevant state and non-state actors such as youth welfare offices and private security companies.

Enjoying standard guidelines and flexibility in approaching diverse societal contexts with adequate set of tools, problem-oriented policing appears to be founded on a sound methodological basis and to be equipped with better-defined courses of action than the rather ambiguous "community policing".[117] Braga and Weisburd[118] nevertheless criticize that while POP seems to be promising in theory, enforcement problem-oriented policing often prevails over "softer" approaches to policing, and the strict compliance to the SARA guidelines are often neglected by police officers.

The Historical Origins of Community Policing in 19th Century Britain and Imperial Japan

This chapter addresses the frequently cited historical origins of the contemporary community policing paradigm. The British *metropolitan policing* by Sir Robert Peel as well as the Japanese *koban* policing are regarded as the main sources of community policing in theoretical as well as in practical terms for contemporary community-based approaches to policing.[119] Moreover, the Peelian police reform and the consequential British metropolitan policing are regarded as the foundation for modern policing.[120]

The paper explicitly takes the respective country context and its normative objectives of police reform into account. Therefore, discussing the British Metropolitan policing and the Imperial Japanese *koban* policing does not intend to equate these political entities with each other. Due to the significance of the Metropolitan policing approach in modern policing, the Metropolitan policing approach serves as the main reference point for the subsequent variances of community policing approaches. While the Peelian police reform will be presented in the first part of this section, the second part takes a closer look at the Japanese *koban* and its development since the late 19th century in Japan. Finally, the last part of this chapter reflects on the creation and development of *koban* policing in light of the theoretical framework. The chapter illustrates, and this is particularly true for the *koban* approach, that closely linked police-citizen relations and cooperation enabled the police to establish a comprehensive and complex surveillance system to uphold state security.

Metropolitan Policing in 19th Century London

The reform of the British police in the 19th century and its developed metropolitan policing model and basic organisational structure influenced police organisations around the globe. The necessity to reform the British police in the early 19th century by Sir Robert Peel was contingent

---

upon substantial societal and economic transformation of the Victorian era. The increasing urbanisation as part of the British industrialisation process brought new challenges to the existing order.[121] The fast-growing urban settlements in Britain were not only accompanied by industrial development, wealth, and prosperity, but also by the development of slums and a rising crime rate. Soon doubts on the professional orientation and effectiveness of the traditional British police to cope with these changes gained weight within the British administration.

The new metropolitan police was more than just a crime-fighting agency; beyond maintaining public order, their assigned tasks revolved around extended dimensions of police work, such as the control and surveillance of the working class and migrated people from the British colonies. Hence, police work did not stop in front of the doorstep but found its way into the people's homes to intervene in cases of alcohol abuse, domestic violence, and as behaviour that was perceived to be deviant from Puritan norms.[122]

The traditional British policing before the Peelian police reforms consisted generally out of untrained and underpaid men from the respective local municipality as well as of a multitude of private-security actors. Their main tasks were the protection and escorting of the local tax collec-tor as well as haunting reported felonies. In addition, recruited residents had to act as "watchmen" by night or as "wards" by day to patrol the streets and detain perceived suspects. The rational bases for these executive actions were generally ad hoc decisions without a solid legal foundation. Frequently, male members of the communities were also called together through a mandatory *hue and cry* to apprehend a criminal suspect. Overall, the character of the traditional, primordial British policing can be described as ineffective and highly reactive since there was actually no rule-based and organized progressive and preventive crime-fighting strategy in place.[123]

The deployment of uniformed policemen who went in regular shifts on patrol in urban bor-oughs should actively prevent crime. In contrast to the traditional policing, then-Home Secretary Sir Robert Peel aimed at a regulated and centralised policing model for Britain. Mayhall,[124] among others, specified nine principles of Sir Robert Peel, which should guide the Metropolitan police in their daily work. A main focus of these very principles appears to be the premise of non-violence as part of the police service. The use of force, as the principles stated, should be the last resort. This aspiration of non-violence is grounded in the understanding that the police are a service for the people and not against the people. Moreover, the principle of rule-based policing should avoid any abuse of power by the Metropolitan police officers.[125]

Concerning the disciplinary regulations, Peel resorted to a military-disciplinary framework. However, unlike the military, the Peelian Metropolitan police did not carry lethal weapons during patrols.[126] British politicians' response was initially hostile to the idea of adopting military disci-pline and military-like uniforms by the metropolitan police. Their main concern was that these measures would lead to a militarisation of the British police similar to the negatively perceived continental, and particularly absolutist French, policing model of the militarised Gendarmerie.[127] Most important, however, hitherto there wasn't any known viable organizational model one could refer to except the military organisational structure. Additionally, the centralised military organi-sational model was unique in its ability to effectively regulate an agency with executive powers and to prevent any deviations from the given rules of engagement.

The uniforms for the Peelian policemen were in so far a novelty as traditional policemen con-ducted their work in plainclothes. To uniform the new police force, however, as Monkkonen[128] argues, was not a sign of exclusiveness or militarisation but a measure to make police officers highly visible and easily approachable by the population. Moreover, Peel's recourse on the military structure as a role model for the new metropolitan police was actually not inspired by the idea to militarise the British police, as several authors argue.[129] It also has to be noted that the Metropoli-tan police was issued blue uniforms while the British military wore the traditional scarlet red coat. This indicated a clear distinction between the military and the police.[130]

Irrespective of the resistance to his policing model, Peel, in his function as Home Secretary, brought the Metropolitan Police Act of 1829 into action. Soon, newly recruited metropolitan policemen patrolled the boroughs of London on a regular basis. While the number of newly recruited metropolitan policemen continuously rose, the Home Secretary opted for a temporary coexistence of traditional policemen, private security actors, and metropolitan police officers until 1840.[131] From the 1830s onwards, the new metropolitan policing model expanded across the country. But despite the Rural Constabulary Act of 1839, which codified the Peelian police reform on the countryside, a nationwide implementation of the police reforms did not take place until the 1850s. Emsley[132] explains this fragmentary implementation of police reforms with the unwillingness of local mayors to cede control over local police forces. More important for the limited police reform, however, was the unwillingness of local policemen to adapt to the new conceptual orientation of the metropolitan policing towards a preventive and proactive style of policing. In many cases, traditional forms of reactive policing prevailed in Britain until the 1890s.

Koban Policing in Imperial Japan

The Western community policing approach has been frequently attributed to the Japanese *koban* policing. To date, the Japanese *koban* acts as prototype for successful community policing.[133] In essence, *koban* policing stands for intensive communication and collaboration between the Japanese police and citizens and is widely regarded as role model and inspiration for police-citizen partnership.

Due to the relatively low crime rates in Japan during the 1970s and 1980s, the Japanese policing approach has been internationally heralded as a role model for its assumed mutually trusting relationship between the police and the population.[134] Bayley's influential book *Forces of Order: Police Behaviour in Japan and the United States*[135] is regarded as the initial spark for the international interest in the Japanese approach to policing. His well-cited book depicts the hitherto relatively unnoticed *koban* policing. According to Bayley, the responsiveness and friendliness of the Japanese *koban* officers constitutes the basis for an amicable relationship between the citizens and the police. Moreover, Bayley stressed the fact that *koban* officers do foot patrols on a regular basis, which enables them to get to know the respective neighbourhood and its residents. It is this constant but unobtrusive police presence on the streets that generates a feeling of safety and protection on behalf of the local residents, as Bayley concluded.[136] Similar to Bayley's book, Vogel[137] reported about the exceptionally low crime rates in Japan in comparison with other industrialized countries and identified *koban* policing as a main reason for this success in crime control. However, a long-time observer of Japanese society stressed even at that time the potential of misuse of power and widespread one-sided intelligence gathering of the Japanese police through its complex networks to neighbourhood associations and the neighbourhood police boxes known as *koban*.[138]

The origins of the *koban* policing approach date back to the Japanese Empire in the late 19th century. The demise of the Togukawa dynasty and the accession to power of Tenno Mutsuhito triggered an extensive modernisation of the Japanese Empire, known as *Meiji* reforms. Alongside the centralisation and professionalization of the bureaucratic apparatus, the Japanese state-building approach also encompassed a thorough reform and build-up of a police force following the example of European police institutions. The Japanese executive's commitment to implement a Western policing approach in Imperial Japan was high; particularly influenced by the European continental policing model, the Japanese Interior Ministry sent officials to Europe but also invited French and German police advisors and practitioners to introduce and implement European continental policing strategies to the Japanese context.[139] Relating to this, it is important to note that the Japanese police build-up was modelled on the British metropolitan policing insofar as the

Japanese police adapted the basic idea of a modernized police with a uniformed police corps acting in line with an elaborated set of regulations. However, since the Japanese leadership aimed at a rigorous state-building agenda and a powerful police force to maintain state security during the far-reaching and comprehensive political and societal reform in Japan, it opted for the centralized and militarily shaped continental policing model, as Aldous[140] stresses.

To enable the Japanese police to be present in every part of the country and to defend the state's monopoly on the use of force, the Japanese Interior Ministry opted for the area-wide installation of police boxes. The installation of these boxes was inspired by the German concept of extensive social control through the police.[141] While *koban* police boxes were mainly established in urban areas, *chuzaisho* police houses were installed in rural parts of the country as the functional equivalent to *koban* boxes. Both the *koban* as well as the *chuzaisho* initially aimed at a thorough control and surveillance of the population and at a closer interaction between the stationed police offers with the nearby residents.[142]

Officers stationed in the *koban* boxes were tasked with assistance in emergency situations but acted also as first contact for residents in case of complaints and reports of criminal acts. Moreover, *koban* police officers registered every resident and regularly conducted mandatory house visits. During these house visits, residents had to provide detailed personal information such as their family status and occupation. While the police officers in the metropolitan areas were only assigned to work during shifts in the *koban* boxes, police officers on the countryside actually lived with their families in the *chuzaisho*. Similar to the *koban* officers, rural *chuzaisho* police officers had comprehensive knowledge on the personal living situations of every resident within their service area and conducted housing visits on a regular basis.[143]

An important feature of the internal security policy in the Japanese Empire was the political and social dimension of policing: The immediate proximity of the police to the Japanese population through *koban* and *chuzaisho* enabled the police not only to represent and defend the state's monopoly on the use of force but also to control the loyalty and subordination of the population to the Imperial political doctrine. In this vein Ramcharan[144] emphasizes the deeply entrenched social hierarchical order and the paternalistic habitus of state officials, such as the police, towards the citizens. The above-mentioned conducted house visits on a regular basis by *koban* officers illustrate how far the surveillance actually went. In addition to the gathered information on the size of each household and the respective dwellers' occupations, the police categorized each resident into a risk group and conducted profiling. While noblemen, landowners, as well as residents with decent professions were visited by *koban* officers only twice a year, residents who were perceived as a potential threat to state security as well as relatively poor people were visited every month by the police. Unemployed residents, former inmates, and politically active residents were visited three times a month.[145] This comprehensive surveillance and intelligence gathering by the Japanese police increased particularly during the Second World War since political activism and deviation from societal standards were perceived as a threat to the government.[146]

Of great importance for the police-citizen cooperation as part of *koban* policing are the Japanese neighbourhood associations (*tonari-gumi*). These neighbourhood associations are deeply entrenched into the Japanese cultural history and date back to the 17th century. According to Aldous[147] and Onda,[148] the *tonari-gumi* acted as "auxiliary police" during the Second World War in mainland Japan. They were actively focussed on maintaining social order and identifying critics of the government within their neighbourhood and to report them to the state authorities. Although not a direct offspring of the *tonari-gumi*, post-war established *Crime Prevention Associations*, organized by local businessmen in cooperation with the local police stations followed a similar strategy as the *tonari-gumi* and display the still-close relationship between the police and the population in Japan.[149] These Crime Prevention Associations try to sensitize the respective residents for potential criminal activities and to prevent crime through showing presence, attentiveness, and even through instructing perceived wrongdoers in public.[150]

The post-war occupation of Japan by the Supreme Commander of the Allied Powers (SCAP) led to comprehensive reforms of the public service and state institutions. Apart from the Imperial Military, the Japanese police system was considered by the American occupying forces as the epitome of the authoritarian und hierarchical Japanese Imperial mindset. Therefore, the SCAP initiated police reforms aimed at the decentralization of the police and a limitation of police powers. One point of criticism on the police's sweeping powers was the detailed personal information each Japanese citizen had to reveal to the *koban* officers. However, despite the reform attempts and the targeted "democratization" of the Japanese police by the American occupying forces, the Japanese police force was able to maintain established practices and ideas of how to police the Japanese society. Still, social control, one-sided intelligence gathering, and tight surveillance, as Aldous[151] argues, were among the primary duties of *koban* officers in post-war Japan. Moreover, changing geopolitical developments during the 1950s caused an end to the formal occupation of Japan by SCAP and enabled the Japanese police to regain their centralized structure just as in the pre-war period.[152]

Still, critical observers perceive the contemporary Japanese *koban* policing first and foremost as a surveillance tool to effectively control the population.[153] While answering the *koban* household surveys is not mandatory anymore, Katzenstein and Tsujinaka[154] argue that refusing to comply with *koban* officers might even appear suspicious to the police officers and arouse the police's curiosity. Even if residents declined to answer the regular surveys, *koban* officers stationed nearby would be able to record movement profiles and additional information with the help of cooperating neighbours and community associations. Even non-resident visitors would be monitored and recorded by *koban* officers in case they were perceived as a potential threat to the community.[155] Moreover, neighbourhood gossip about unpopular residents who are not socially integrated into the neighbourhood community might also be forwarded to *koban* officers and appear on the records, fostering immense pressure on individualists.[156] Furthermore, the gathered data on each resident is not exclusively kept in the local *koban* boxes but accessible to other state agencies in case a profile attracts attention and fits to perceived risk groups.[157]

The Japanese *koban* policing emerged during a phase of enormous social and political transformation. Traditional reactive police forces were not able to cope with the pace of societal development and concomitant challenges regarding the operational area, nor did they have the necessary professional tools and knowledge. Moreover, the introduction of a modern police force in Imperial Japan has been regarded on behalf of the political leadership as one of several epitomes of modern statehood. Hence, local ownership and commitment in supporting the reform of the police was crucial. As part of a modernization and state-building project, an effectively operating police organization was tasked with the provision of state security in rural and urban areas.

Ames's quotation perfectly defines the theoretical underpinnings of this paper on adaptation, reinterpretation, and resistance when he describes the Japanese *koban* policing as "blended amalgam of the authoritarian, powerful, and highly centralized prewar police system and the 'democratic' and decentralized post-war system."[158] Hence, the Japanese *koban* is not a solely Japanese creation but an outcome of exactly the above-mentioned adaptation processes between external and local approaches to policing. The case study on the formation of *koban* policing in Japan therefore answers the initial research questions regarding the historical origins of community policing as well as the necessary conditions to establish a community-oriented approach to policing.

To become explicit: The implementation of foreign approaches to policing and the creation of *koban* policing as a very local approach to policing was driven by a strong local ownership and a clear political agenda. During an era in Japanese history with major socio-political transformations, the Japanese political leadership actively sought for external or foreign modes of policing in order to maintain state security. The general modern concept of policing introduced by Peel through the metropolitan policing approach, as well as the highly centralized and bureaucratized continental approach to policing, fit the Japanese demand for effective regulated policing. Due to the existence of a strong local ownership and commitment on behalf of the Japanese political leadership, the external model was soon adapted and combined with the traditional Japanese hierarchical and paternalistic norms and values as well as with the traditional local cooperation patterns between the police and neighbourhood associations, the *tonari-gumi*, to expand the police's surveillance capacities. Particularly this reinterpretation or alteration of an external concept on behalf of the local leadership to a very own concept, as De La Rosa[159] and Draude[160] describe it, eventually facilitate the implementation process in the local context. Moreover, the thorough implementation of a professional bureaucratic police system with rigidly minded rules and regulations enabled an unimpeded continuation of police development and practice in Japan.

Bringing the Community Policing Paradigm to Singapore and Timor-Leste

Conveying community policing approaches to post-conflict settings and countries in political transition became a prominent strategy by international development agencies and donor countries because community policing has been interpreted as a most suitable tool to overcome police brutality and human rights abuses by local security forces. Implementing the concept of community policing, as the official narrative goes, would help the respective country to adopt an international best-practice approach to improve police-community relationships, and eventually, to foster societal peace.

Due to the propagated success of community policing in the United States and other Western countries, community policing became part of a political reform package for developing and transitional countries. According to Brogden,[161] community policing had been uncritically presented as a particularly suitable tool for post-conflict and post-authoritarian societies in their attempts to leave behind the often brutal and inhuman policing practices of the former autocratic governments. Also, donor countries, the United Nations, and other international development agencies incorporated the theme of community policing into their programs and even advertised community policing as the "best-practice" to cope with rising crime rates in the respective transitional countries.[162] Moreover, as several authors[163] add for consideration, development program funds were increasingly linked and even conditioned to the successful implementation of community policing into the national police structures of developing countries. The United Nations Transitional Administration in Timor-Leste (UNTAET), for instance, issued the implementation of community policing as a guiding policing principle in Timor-Leste for the to-be-established national police.[164] The rationale behind this idea was Timor-Leste's presumed cultural proximity to Japan and Singapore. The successful Implementation of community-oriented policing similar to the Japanese *koban* and the Singaporean *community policing system (COPS)* in an Asian country, so the assumption went, would be quite likely.[165]

How to cite this book chapter:
Kocak, D. 2018. *Rethinking Community Policing in International Police Reform: Examples from Asia.* Pp. 23–32. London: Ubiquity Press. DOI: https://doi.org/10.5334/bcb.e. License: CC-BY 4.0

In the course of several years, an international network of community policing experts evolved. Private security companies and contractors such as DynCorp were assigned by the United Nations to conduct community policing training courses in several UN-mission countries.[166] Despite the large pool of international experts, who were mostly recruited out of retired military and police-men, as well as the comprehensive financial support to implement community policing in volatile contexts, guidance of how to actually implement community policing mainly rested on standard measures and recommendations such as the establishment of community fora or advisory boards, the creation of beat officers and foot patrols, a decentralization of the police and enhanced discre-tion to officers on the beat, the establishment of small police stations similar to the *koban* police box within the communities as well as community watch programs, and often vaguely formulated plans for police-public partnerships.[167] While these measures do in fact mirror the internationally supported best-practice guidelines of how to promote community policing in developing coun-tries, the local historical and socio-political contexts of the respective countries were usually not taken into consideration, leaving behind hardly compatible local institutional bodies.[168]

This chapter will take a closer look at the actual implementation of the community policing approach in Singapore during the 1980s and in Timor-Leste since 2000. Singapore is neither a developing country nor a country in political transition. However, Singapore is one of the few non-Western cases where community policing has been adapted in a successful way. Moreover, the case of Singapore builds a direct causal link between the Japanese *koban* policing and the United Nation's envisaged approach to policing in Timor-Leste.[169]

The Southeast Asian city-state with a non-democratic hegemonic party[170] system experienced considerable economic development since its independence in the 1960s. This fast pace of eco-nomic development and thorough societal change is of particular interest because economic and societal change also affects the political architecture and stability of a country.[171] In fact, the Singaporean administration perceived the multi-ethnic composition of the newly built high-rise residential quarters as a potential threat to political stability.[172] Hence, the implementation of com-munity policing aimed first and foremost at state security and enhanced techniques to maintain public order. This government-driven and locally owned implementation of a community-oriented approach to policing during the 1980s, initially modelled after the Japanese *koban*, has been principally treated as a success story. Moreover, in the course of ten years, the Singaporean community-oriented policing version of the Japanese *koban* became an integral part of policing in the city-state.

Reviewing the case of Singapore will give important insights into necessary and sufficient conditions in order to promote and develop an environment conducive to community-oriented policing. Therefore, the first part of this chapter will take a closer look at Singapore's actual community policing implementation process in the 1980s and 1990s, its promises, and its results.

This is followed by a case study on the development of community policing in Timor-Leste. Due to the comprehensive international support after the Indonesian retreat from Timor-Leste in 1999, the extensive political and legal powers of the United Nations Transitional Administra-tion in Timor-Leste (UNTAET), Timor-Leste has been regarded as one of the most ideal places to successfully implement community policing due to the fact that the police had to be built from scratch, with the comprehensive political and technical powers of UNTAET. Yet, by reflecting the overall programmatic aims of the international donors, the actual implementation process, its stagnation, as well as recent strategic changes regarding how to foster the understanding of community policing within the Timorese police, it becomes clear that police reform towards community-oriented policing is not a straightforward process but heavily relies on adaptation processes, local ownership, and a functioning local police institution with basic police practice and knowledge in the first place.

Implementing Community Policing in Singapore

The city-state of Singapore introduced the concept of community policing as one of the main pillars of policing in the 1980s. Due to the overall economic development of the semi-authoritarian city-state, the rapidly changing housing situation of the Singaporeans and the establishment of large apartment blocks managed by the Singaporean Housing and Development Board (HDB), these densely populated and multi-ethnic housing complexes posed a challenge for the public order and societal peace. While the Singaporean police was fully operational in terms of law-enforcement capabilities due to the British colonial rule and its concomitant focus on professional bureaucratic capacity building,[173] its traditional reactive approach to policing, also inherited by the British colonial forces, was not able to cope with the rapid social and demographic changes in Singapore. Therefore, new strategies to contain the rising criminality in the apartment complexes and to effectively represent state authority by the police were sought after by the Singaporean administration.[174]

In search of new approaches to policing, Singaporean decision makers became aware of the growing trend to perceive the highly industrialized Japan as model for successful state development. Scholarly monographs, such as the book *Japan as Number One: Lessons for America* by Ezra Vogel,[175] underpinned the mainstream media in this assumption.[176] Moreover, David H. Bayley's[177] monograph on the successful Japanese police approach supported the narrative of Japan as a high-technology country but with strong adherence to traditional Asian values and a virtually crimeless and peaceful society even more.

The Japanese *koban* policing seemed to be the most promising model to police Singapore, given the then relatively low crime rates and the high crime clearance rate in Japan; a fact which has been increasingly scrutinized since the 1990s and even called a myth.[178] Moreover, as Ramcharan[179] points out, *koban* policing had a special appeal to Singaporean policy makers since *koban* policing promised to deliver more than just policing but had also a strong ability for social surveillance – a factor not to underestimate to maintain state security in a relatively newly founded city-state surrounded by Malaysia and Indonesia, two perceived potential invaders.[180]

To introduce community policing in Singapore and to learn about the mechanisms and techniques of this policing approach, the city-state's administration organised and promoted several study tours for police officers and bureaucrats to Japan. Moreover, the Japan International Cooperation Agency (JICA) became active in Singapore during the early 1980s to facilitate *koban* policing for Singaporean police officials and to train Singaporean police officers in community policing techniques.[181] As a result, the Singaporean police introduced their first "Neighbourhood Police Posts" (NPP) in 1983. These NPP, based on the idea of the Japanese *koban* boxes, were responsible for nearby housing complexes. It was the stated aim of the Singaporean police that the introduction of the NPP should foster trust between the residents and the police, to reduce crime, and that the NPP officer should set an example of civic duties and values in daily life for the HDB residents.[182]

NPP officers conducted their service along several lines of strategy: For one, NPP officers aimed at improved police-community relations and signalled approachability through constant visibility on the complex compounds as well as through foot patrol. Moreover, the police approached local neighbourhood associations and nearby civil-society organisations to establish cooperation regarding the organisation of awareness campaigns and the formation of neighbourhood watches.[183] The NPP officers also started comprehensive outreach programs particularly targeted at youths. Daily youth clubs were aimed at teaching juveniles how to avoid conflicts and advising them not to get involved into youth gang business. These workshops and youth clubs were organized and run by NPP officers as well as volunteers from the nearby HDB complexes.[184] Furthermore, the Singaporean administration started comprehensive awareness campaigns on the role of the reformed police and the necessity for each citizen to fight crime in cooperation with the police to ultimately achieve a safer Singapore.[185]

Based on the *koban* policing, NPP officers also conducted house visits to all the HDB residents. House visits functioned as starting point for police-citizen approximation in general, but also as possibility to gather information on the respective residents, their living circumstances, and additional information on the neighbourhood.[186] While NPP were regular police, NPP regulations did not allow executing arrests. As a reaction to the criticism by police officers and politicians regarding the limited executive powers of the NPP officers, the NPP were replaced by the "Neighbourhood Police Centres" (NPC) in 1997. Unlike the previous NPP officers, the NPC officers had extended executive powers such as making arrests and conducting police investigations. Moreover, the establishment of the more centralized NPC were a reaction to the ongoing urban growth. By centralizing the community policing service and co-locating NPC officers in Community Centres, the police gained better access to the respective communities in order to organize crime prevention and awareness campaigns and programmes.[187]

Overall, the introduction of the NPP scheme meant a departure from reactive policing. Moreover, the Singaporean approach to community policing was perceived as a success and a possibility for strengthening the police-citizen relations. As a result, Singaporeans participated in crime-prevention programmes organized by the NPP and later the NPC in collaboration with the Community Centres. Thang and Gan[188] report an increase in police-citizen cooperation due to improved communication channels and trust in the police in general on behalf of the citizens.

Similar to the adaptation of European continental modes of policing in 19th century Imperial Japan and the local creation of *koban* policing, the implementation process of the Japanese *koban* in Singapore during the 1980s also features elements of adaptation and local reinterpretation to create a local version of community policing.

Due to rapid economic development and socio-political transformations, the administration of the densely populated multi-ethnic city-state sought new approaches to policing. To ensure political and social order, the Singaporean political leadership sought suitable solutions for how to reduce the overall crime in the city-state and to maintain public order. The most promising approach for this endeavour seemed to the Japanese *koban*. Driven by the political will and commitment for change, the Singaporean political leadership promoted the implementation of *koban* in Singapore and its adaptation to the local context. Therefore, the established Neighbourhood Police Posts (NPP) in the large apartment blocks and concomitant police initiatives to prevent crime represent a very own version of *koban* in Singapore. It has to be noted that, in contrast to the relatively ethnic homogenous society in Japan, Singapore is a multi-ethnic society with parallel existing cultural and religious normative concepts. Therefore, a local reinterpretation of the external *koban* approach was a necessity to be applicable to the Singaporean context. Yet, driven by a broad local ownership and the necessary bureaucratic police capacity, the Singaporean version of *koban* succeeded and even experienced an adjustment in 1997 with extended executive powers to the Neighbourhood Police Centres (NPCs).

Implementing Community Policing in Timor-Leste

In line with the general international trend of perceiving community-based policing as the most suitable tool to overcome police brutality in conflict-affected and transitional societies, the United Nations as well as several international donors aimed at the implementation of community policing in Timor-Leste after its independence from Indonesia and the military intervention of INTERFET troops in 1999.

The case of Timor-Leste is considered as a crucial case regarding the external implementation of police reforms in post-conflict scenarios because the country was entrusted to the United Nations Transitional Administration in East Timor (UNTAET) during the transitional phase between

1999 and 2002. At that time, UNTAET had comprehensive legal, executive, and judicial powers at its disposal. In this position, UNTAET enacted several regulations on the establishment of the Timorese police and the Timorese armed forces, outlining their composition, tasks, and directions, respectively. Furthermore, UNTAET was one of the most comprehensive missions of the United Nations with one of the highest manning levels.[189] However, due to its Portuguese colonial legacy as well as its twenty-five-year incorporation into the unitary state of Indonesia until 1999, Timor-Leste never experienced rule-based and accountable policing. Contrary to the British colonial state-building activities in mainland Southeast Asia, the Portuguese colonial rulers did not seek to create viable bureaucratic apparatuses in their occupied overseas territories. Particularly then, Portuguese Timor was chronically underfunded and misgoverned. Militarized forces policed the settlements and the countryside at discretion.[190] Hence, the concept of a police service working along the lines of binding legal regulations and human rights, let alone the concept of policing as a public good, was non-existent.

As illustrated in the first section of this chapter, the implementation of community policing by the United Nations in Timor-Leste followed the assumption that Timor-Leste, as an Asian country, would easily and successfully adapt the guiding principles of community policing, as Singapore did in the 1980s.[191] However, contrary to the donor's expectations, a community-oriented approach to policing in line with liberal democratic values did not materialize in Timor-Leste, even after ten years of independence. Only recently have instances of community-oriented policing emerged in several rural districts of the country.

The increasing attractiveness of community policing within international policy circles since the mid-1990s, as well as the general assumption that community policing would improve police-citizen relations in post-conflict and transitional countries, influenced the United Nations to declare community policing as the intended policing approach in independent Timor-Leste. Mandated by the United Nations Security Council[192] in 1999 with executive, legislative, and judicial powers, UNTAET soon started to establish a local police force in Timor-Leste.[193] According to the United Nations General Secretary,[194] and in line with the overall goal of implementing a community-based approach to policing in Timor-Leste, the United Nations Police (UNPOL) was advised to execute community policing in Timor-Leste. However, apart from a lecture about community policing during the pre-deployment training for UNPOL officers, precise specifications and terms of reference for how to uniformly conduct community policing in Timor-Leste were not issued by the United Nations. Ambiguous specifications concerning the proposed policing approach in Timor-Leste, combined with the heterogeneous composition of UNPOL, with more than forty contributing countries, therefore led to an overall confusion as to how to ultimately police the post-conflict country.[195]

As a result, UNPOL officers conducted community policing according to their very own interpretations about community policing. In one case, a group of UNPOL officers stayed with their PNTL counterparts in the police station and abstained from going on patrol or making contact with the nearby residents since the officers' understanding of community policing revolved around the idea that the community should solve problems on their own without the assistance of the police. In another case, UNPOL officers organized various small-scale sporting events in their policing districts to establish contacts between the Timorese police and youth groups living nearby.[196]

Apart from the United Nations' police-building activities, several bilateral donors engaged in implementing community policing in Timor-Leste, particularly Japan, Australia, and New Zealand.[197] Since 2001, Japan promoted community policing through JICA in Timor-Leste. As part of the training program, JICA regularly organized educational tours for Timorese police officers in Japan to learn about *koban* policing and to get an idea of the Japanese approach to police-citizen relationships.[198]

Despite the offered training programs for Timorese police officers, however, there were sceptical voices, even within JICA, on the actual feasibility of implementing community policing as the main approach to policing in Timor-Leste; while some Timorese police officers eventually embraced the community policing approach as a possibility for fostering police-citizen relationships, the majority of PNTL officers would still reject this "soft" approach to policing and vehemently question its utility and applicability to the Timorese context.[199]

As another bilateral donor, the New Zealand Police engaged in promoting community policing in Timor-Leste. Apart from supporting the then–United Nations mission[200] in its attempt to implement a community-oriented policing approach in Timor-Leste since 2002 the New Zealand Police also conducted a pilot project on community policing support from 2008 to 2010 in selected districts. Moreover, the Australian Federal Police (AFP) promoted community policing as part of the Timor-Leste Police Development Programme (TLPDP) since 2004. The declared aim of both projects was not to present community policing as a foreign policing model to the Timorese police and the population but rather to exemplify the benefits of community-oriented police work in practice and to communicate the underlying philosophy of community policing to the participating PNTL officers.[201]

Officially, community policing has been supported by the Timorese police command and the political leadership through public statements and police internal regulations. In this respect the Timorese administration fully complied with the requirements of the bilateral and multilateral donors to implement community policing in Timor-Leste. However, there has been an increasing subtle resistance to international demands on police reform, and actual alterations within the Timorese police rather appeared as mere tactical concessions to maintain the internationally funded support to the Timorese police.[202]

One of the main steps to implement the community policing approach within the Timorese police was the formation of the Community Policing Department (Departementu Policiamento Comunitário) within the PNTL General Command based on the PNTL Organic Law of 2009.[203] The department is officially tasked with planning and programming of community policing activities within the PNTL, the active communication of community policing activities of the PNTL to the public as well as the support of rural police stations in implementing community policing.

Long-time national and international observers, however, questioned the actual willingness of the political leadership and the police command to thoroughly implement community policing as the main policing approach in Timor-Leste because community policing still has been perceived as a "soft", ineffective, and alien approach to policing.[204] Meaningful local ownership regarding the implementation of a community-oriented approach to policing was therefore missing within the Timorese political leadership.

Moreover, conflicts between the Timorese police and the Timorese armed forces (*Falintil-Forças de Defesa de Timor Leste (F-FDTL)*) about areas of responsibility for internal security might also have had an impact on the decision of the police command not to follow a thorough implementation of community policing. According to this reasoning, a comprehensive implementation of community policing within the PNTL would curtail the police's ability for robust policing and yield the floor for permanent deployments in the field internal security to the F-FDTL,[205] an outcome which would counter the United Nations' aspirations of establishing a clear-cut role allocation for the Timorese armed forces with a definite focus on external security, and for the police with the sole focus on internal security.[206] Additionally, there has been broad resistance, particularly within lower echelons of the PNTL, to approaches to policing perceived as "soft" and "unmanly". Moreover, as an UN official confirmed,[207] there is an undisputed perception that effective policing is based on dominance, assertiveness, and the display of weapons to gain compliance on behalf of the citizens.

According to the commander of the community policing department, the community policing officers conduct house visits, hold meetings with traditional *suco* leaders, and visit schools to promote community policing and good relations between the police and the population on a regular basis. Moreover, the department is responsible for teaching other PNTL units community policing techniques and ensuring that there is a general understanding of community policing within the PNTL.[208] A local NGO, however, despite being supportive to the overall development of the community policing approach in Timor-Leste, argued that there is no satisfying commitment on behalf of PNTL officers to promote police-citizen cooperation.[209] Given the limited manning level of the community policing department of around nine police officers only,[210] and measured against the total PNTL-manning level of approximately 3,400 officers in 2012, it is no surprise that community policing has had a limited impact at all.

Realizing the difficulties of implementing community policing as the main policing approach in Timor-Leste as well as the increasing resistance to the community policing approach by the local political leadership, the Australian TLPDP altered its strategy from conducting general community policing classes to a focussed supporting programme for mid-level officers only.[211] Led by the insight that the context of Australian policing cannot be simply transferred to Timor-Leste, the TLPDP rather aimed at a sustained training in three core areas: police management and leadership, investigations, and administration.[212]

The adjusted strategy of the TLPDP explicitly aimed at a sustained mindset change from within the mid-level police management. The Australian approach to police reform towards reflective, communication-based and problem-oriented policing in Timor-Leste therefore had to depart from the dogmatic understanding of simply implementing standardized best-practice toolkits to a different country context.[213] Instead of promoting a relatively vague policing concept with relatively little compatibility to the actual Timorese policing experience, the TLPDP's strategy rather fell back to teaching the very foundations of basic police practice and knowledge.

The successor program of the New Zealand Police in Timor-Leste started in 2011 and was executed in collaboration with the Asia Foundation. While the "Timor-Leste Community Policing Programme" (TLCPP) of the New Zealand Police focussed on community policing-related training of Timorese police officers, such as mentoring in communication strategies with the population as well as public outreach, the Asia Foundation component ("Conflict Mitigation Through Community-Oriented Policing Programme") organized awareness campaigns and communication training for traditional *suco* councils.[214] The training manuals of the TLCPP programme and Asia Foundation for the Timorese police[215] relied basically on standard measures of Problem-Oriented Policing such as the SARA tool. Furthermore, the training programs focussed rather on hands-on recommendations for basic police work and communication strategies than on a rigid guidance of theoretical underpinnings of community policing. The declared aim of the programme was to present community policing not as a foreign approach to policing with limited relevance to the Timorese context but as a highly effective and feasible approach to policing based on a sound partnership between the police and the population.[216]

As part of a second step in implementing community policing in Timor-Leste, New Zealand's TLCCP and the Asia Foundation approached the district police commands and the respective communities. By establishing more than one hundred community police councils in the districts and by closely mentoring community policing officers, both the local police as well as the community members approached each other and increased police-citizen communication.[217]

Moreover, the commander of the Timorese Community Policing Department reformulated the overall community policing strategy for the Timorese police and created the so-called V.I.P approach (*Visibility, Involvement, and Professionalism*). As part of this new community policing approach, community policing officers in the sub-districts (*Ofisial Polísia Suku*, OPS) were explicitly charged with taking part in council meetings and increased communication with the community members.[218] Officially, the PNTL command embraces the notion of serving the people of Timor-Leste and reiterates in the PNTL Strategic Plan 2014–2018 the objective of adopting the

V.I.P. approach not only in the Community Policing Department but in all units and departments of the PNTL.[219]

In fact, the Timorese approach to community-oriented policing is not only the outcome of the recent donor initiatives by the Australian and New Zealand police-development programmes in cooperation with the Asia Foundation alone, but also rests on Timorese experiences during the Indonesian occupation (1975–1999).[220] When the Japanese Imperial Armed Forces invaded the then–Dutch East Indies (today's Indonesia), they also transferred known tools and models of surveillance and control. To secure the Indonesian peninsula, the Japanese occupying administration made use of the Japanese system of neighbourhood watches (*tonari gumi*)[221] and functional equivalents to the rural *chuzaisho* policing posts. According to Sebastian,[222] the Japanese even combined the *tonari-gumi* neighbourhood watch system with traditional Javanese watch systems (*gotong royong*) to strengthen the effectiveness of their surveillance and control measures. Furthermore, as Sebastian explains, the Japanese techniques of surveillance and community control were adopted by the Indonesian authorities after the Indonesian independence in 1949, and applied in the course of the Indonesian state-building endeavours across the vast Indonesian archipelago.[223]

Due to the Indonesian dual-function doctrine (*dwifungsi*), which allowed the Indonesian military extensive powers in security as well as socio-political affairs, and in combination with the "Total People's Defence and Security System" (*Sistem Pertahanan Meanmanan Rakyat Semesta-Sistem Hankamrata*), the military was able to establish parallel administrative structures to the civilian authorities in all provinces of the country.[224] On the village level, the Indonesian military established the Babinsa (*Bintara Pembina Desa*) parallel to the local police, the Bimpolda (*Bimbingan Polisi Desa*). Particularly in then-occupied Timor-Leste the Indonesian authorities used the Babinsa and Bimpolda to gather intelligence through active monitoring and surveillance of the respective community, by taking part in traditional *suco* councils and to single out potential resistance fighters.[225] In essence, the Japanese *tonari-gumi* and the Indonesian Babinsa/Bimpolda policing were first and foremost used as tools to control and surveil the population by an autocratic government.[226] Hence, due to this legacy of community-integrated policing in Timor-Leste, a high ranking PNTL officer who also worked as Bimpolda during Indonesian rule equated the technical approach of community policing in post-independent Timor-Leste most notably with gathering information about the population.[227] Moreover, a PNTL officer who works as OPS even stated that he does not see a difference between the Bimpolda and Babinsa policing and the current OPS approach in Timor-Leste at all.[228]

So far, the present OPS policing approach in Timor-Leste's districts received positive appraisal from community members and police officers alike. While community members perceived the OPS as qualified mediators in cases of communal conflicts as well as in conflicts between sub-districts and state authorities, a recent study by the Asia Foundation also highlighted an increased number of civilians approaching the police instead of customary elites in cases of hardship. Timorese now increasingly address the OPS knowing that their concern is taken care of.[229] Likewise, several interviewed police officers in the sub-districts stated a perceived trust of the respective community members in the sub-district police since the installation of OPS in their districts.[230]

However, despite the positive development regarding the implementation of OPS in the districts and increased trust of the district communities into the police, the OPS are understaffed and ill-equipped. Due to the poor manning level of OPS in the sub-districts, available OPS regularly have to cover more than one community and travel, also due to the bad infrastructure, several hours to reach their destination.[231] Moreover, while OPS improved police-citizen relationships in several districts, successful OPS policing in the capital, Dili, has not materialized yet. Several local NGOs in Dili indicated that neither the regular PNTL nor OPS ever contacted them or anyone in the neighbourhood regarding the introduction of the novel V.I.P. community policing approach.[232] While the director of a local NGO[233] assumes that the absence of OPS in the *sukos* of Dili is caused by the fragmented social ethnic composition in the capital and concomitant difficulties in approaching the respective communities by OPS, international police advisers stationed in Timor-Leste rather see the general unwillingness of police officers in Dili as the main reason for the lack of successful police-citizen cooperation, an assessment several police officers in Dili also confirmed.[234]

Despite comprehensive international support, the implementation of community policing in Timor-Leste has been – and still is – a dragging process. The United Nations' assumption of being able to implement a community-oriented approach to policing in Timor-Leste similar to the Singaporean model failed due to several reasons.

First, the United Nations and several bilateral donors did not take into account the established modes and approaches in Timor-Leste during the Portuguese colonial era as well as during the Indonesian occupation. Both occupiers relied mainly on reactive, repressive, and militarized approaches to policing.[235] Since then, the Timorese population rather feared the police and did not trust the security forces; the general perception of the police on behalf of the Timorese, even after the independence of Timor-Leste in 2002, was rather negative.

Secondly, the United Nations and bilateral donors had to establish a Timorese police institution after the Indonesian retreat in 1999. The actual police building by the United Nations Police (UNPOL) faced harsh criticism due to inexperienced trainers and politicized recruiting procedures.[236] Hence, the national Timorese police resorted to established practices of reactive and militarized policing once the main training initiatives by the UNPOL ended. Moreover, the Timorese police still lack elementary police practice and knowledge skills.[237] These above-mentioned factors impede a service-oriented police service towards the Timorese population, let alone a community-oriented approach to policing.

However, while the introduction of OPS as community-oriented approach to policing in rural areas is a promising sign for police reform in Timor-Leste, there are still reported instances of police brutality and impunity within the Timorese security sector.[238] Hence, a thorough implementation of community policing in Timor-Leste requires not only a thorough mindset change within the Timorese police and the willingness to actually serve the people, but also a consolidation of basic police practice and knowledge and the availability of necessary equipment in all districts.

Contrary to the discussed cases of Japan and Singapore, the implementation of a community-oriented approach to policing in Timor-Leste faced several difficulties.

Timor-Leste holds a legacy of police brutality and human rights violations during the Portuguese and Indonesian occupations of the half-island. Moreover, the withdrawal of the Indonesian occupying forces in 1999 left the country with no institutionalised police in place. However, Timor-Leste also experienced instances of community policing during the Indonesian occupation phase, from 1975 to 1999. The Indonesian authorities implemented a concept of community control and surveillance on the village level in Timor-Leste, a concept the Indonesians themselves learned, adapted, and reinterpreted from the Japanese Imperial Army and their occupation of the Indonesian archipelago during World War II. On the conceptual basis of the Japanese *koban* and the *tonari-gumi* neighbourhood watch system, the Indonesian authorities created the *Babinsa* and *Bimpolda* to gather intelligence in the Timorese communities and to identify potential pockets of resistance and clandestine networks. However, this approach to community policing in the Timorese villages first and foremost aimed at state security of the occupying administration and was not to the benefit of the people. Therefore, this community policing approach was perceived by the local population as a factor of insecurity rather than security. Moreover, due to this negative experience of community policing in Timor-Leste in an authoritarian context, it is challenging for local and external police reformers to rewrite the community policing narrative towards a liberal-democratic concept of policing that adheres to inherent SSR principles and good governance.

While the local police build-up from scratch by the United Nations and several international donors between 2000 and 2002 provided a unique window of opportunity to create the foundations for an accountable, human rights abiding, community-oriented police service in Timor-Leste, practices of brutality and abuse of power by the police against Timorese civilians remained.[239]

Comprehensive financial- and technical support by the United Nations and several international donors to promote and to implement community-oriented policing did not lead to a sustained police reform in Timor-Leste. Rather, subtle or even passive resistance on behalf of the Timorese police and political leadership towards the externally "imposed" concept of policing prevailed, nurtured by the perception that this concept of policing is "inapplicable" to the local context. While the necessary local ownership regarding the implementation of rule-based and human rights oriented policing was missing, the Timorese political leadership instead showed commitment and ownership in establishing and boosting robust and specialized police units. Moreover, missing overall bureaucratic police professionalism and capacity accompanied by grave instances of impunity for police abuse of power due to missing internal oversight functions gave way to shattered police-community relations in Timor-Leste.

This time, a necessary adaptation process to foster a community-oriented approach – or at least basic patterns of basic police practice and knowledge – in Timor-Leste were launched by foreign donors. Realizing the continuing resistance towards a Western-driven community-oriented approach to policing on behalf of local decision makers, the Australian TLDPD, the New Zealand TLCPP, and the Asia Foundation opted for a revision and adjustment to the local realities. Understanding that a sophisticated approach to policing, such as community policing, needs to rest on a solid foundation of basic police practice and knowledge, the adjusted reform approach focussed on basic but sustained mentoring of police professionalism, capacity, and accountability. Apparently, basic policing was the single common denominator between the Timorese legacy of policing and external police reform concepts, such as community policing. Therefore, building on this common ground enabled foreign donors to reach their Timorese counterparts and to incrementally promote a rule-based, accountable, and human rights oriented approach to policing. Eventually, as the establishment of the OPS, the Timorese version of a community policing officer, suggests, instances of a local ownership within the Timorese police towards the promotion of community policing in Timor-Leste emerged.

Conclusions and Recommendations

The paper traced the historical origins of community policing, analysed transfer, implementation, and adaptation processes of approaches to community policing in Imperial Japan, Singapore, and Timor-Leste, and identified supporting as well as obstructive variables to the establishment of community policing. Each of the cases studies provided insights on necessary preconditions for the facilitation of reform towards the implementation of community policing but also highlighted country-specific dynamics and developments of how to adapt to or interpret imported governance concepts. This chapter compares, synthesizes, and discusses the case studies' main findings and provides answers to the initial research questions on the actual historical origins of present-day community policing, the necessary conditions to establish community policing, and the possibility for promoting community policing along the lines of good governance and SSR in developing and transitional countries.

Fostering Community Policing by Building Basic Police Capacities and Supporting Incremental Organizational Change

As the empirical case studies suggest, community-oriented policing is not per se a tool for policing in line with the normative goals of SSR and good governance. Rather, techniques of community-oriented policing have also been used to establish thorough one-sided information networks and surveillance mechanisms to gather in-depth information about the respective communities. This has been particularly true in scenarios of rapid socio-political and economic change in autocratic political systems (19th century Imperial Japan, Singapore) and cases of repressive foreign occupation (Imperial Japan in occupied Indonesia and Indonesia in occupied Timor-Leste). The main security concerns in these scenarios revolved primarily around state security rather than people's security.

How to cite this book chapter:
Kocak, D. 2018. *Rethinking Community Policing in International Police Reform: Examples from Asia.*
Pp. 33–37. London: Ubiquity Press. DOI: https://doi.org/10.5334/bcb.f. License: CC-BY 4.0

In light of the empirical findings, an immediate continuity from the often-cited origins of community policing to an aspired contemporary community-oriented approach to policing that corresponds to a liberal democratic system cannot be attested without restrictions. An uncritical and ahistorical appraisal of community-oriented approaches to policing as a best-practice model to overcome shattered police-community relations in post-conflict and transitional countries would therefore miss the point.

But as the empirical case studies also suggest, community policing works in places where there is a functioning and professional executive body acting according to rigid regulations. The discussed case of Singapore is paradigmatic in this respect. The government-driven and directed implementation of the Japanese approach to community policing is a clear indication of local ownership. Secondly, the Singaporean police was able to adopt the approach to community-oriented policing due to its existing bureaucratic professionalism acquired through its British legacy of administrative and organisational capacity building.[240]

Hence, a sustained implementation of community-oriented policing which finds support not only on behalf of the local administration and the executive security agencies but also on behalf of the local communities, needs to be built on already existing police institutions with experience in bureaucratic professionalism. Particularly the establishment of internal control and accountability mechanisms is key to ensure rule-based and human rights oriented courses of action on behalf of police officers. Alternatively, executing sudden and all-encompassing police reform with the aim of establishing community policing as a guiding principle in a scenario where basic police practice and knowledge, accountability, and rule of law are more or less non-existent due to legacies of police brutality, is unsustainable and unrewarding. In these scenarios, meaningful and tailored capacity building initiatives complemented by comprehensive institutional-reform measures will introduce incremental but sustained change in policing.

Again, it has to be stressed that governance concepts cannot be transferred one-to-one to different cultural environments, but need to be adjusted to the specific country context. The adaptation process should ideally be driven and championed by local authorities to ensure a genuine local commitment and ownership. External actors can support – but cannot impose – the introduction of a particular element or concept. Different ideas and perceptions of the implementation process or the actual outcome may always exist. But external donors have to accept the fact that a local reinterpretation of the external concept and its adjustment to the local way of thinking is a necessary process of intercultural transfers, as the discussed case studies and existing research indicate. Draude highlights this dilemma when she argues that the increase of local ownership leads to the fact that external donors have to change their expectations.[241] To what extent external donors are willing to accept deviations from the actual concept is, of course, subject to their respective policies and agendas.

The ambivalent and uncritical equation of community policing with the concept of democratic policing not only dilutes different concepts of policing but also aggravates the actual implementation of police reform initiatives in a given country due to visionary expectations on the feasibility of the reform process as well as on its ultimate outcome. Therefore, it is indispensable to provide the fundament of basic and professional bureaucratic policing skills in a given country, first through specially programmed capacity building measures. Building on this "core policing", as Bayley and Perito[242] put it, will enable the local police to establish basic policing services to the communities and to incrementally expand their repertoire to more complex approaches of how to interact with the population and how to deal with violence and crime. However, it is particularly important for a post-conflict scenario to promote and to initiate a *mindset* change of the police leadership and its mid-level management to enable sustained commitment for reform and police work in line with SSR inherent norms, provisions, and values. Since SSR is explicitly connected to Western liberal norms and values, a local mindset change towards the acceptance of these very normative values is inevitable.

As long as there is no basic police practice and knowledge in place, international police reform initiatives in cooperation with the local police force will have a hard time identifying a necessary point of leverage to actually initiate the intended reform measures. Insisting on the unconditional implementation of highly normative provisions of good governance and SSR by external donors before establishing a professionally working police body will not bring the anticipated change but might trigger local resistance or indifference instead. But building basic capacities and supporting incremental organizational change in collaboration with the necessary ownership of local authorities within a normative framework of good governance will eventually lay foundations for a starting point to promote the implementation of more complex reforms.

This long-term prospect of police reform efforts admittedly collides with the rather narrow funding cycles of international and national donor missions and programmes. But rethinking donor programmes in terms of long-term commitment would definitely help to make a difference.

Necessary Conditions to Establish Community Policing

The case studies' main findings suggest that a pluralistic and democratic political system is not necessarily needed to establish community policing. In general, the necessary conditions to establish community policing are rather a police organization with, at least, basic professional bureaucratic capacities, a genuine commitment and political will on behalf of local authorities to promote and push for its implementation, and a concept or approach to community policing that actually matters to the respective local context and its realities. Ideally, this approach to community policing is devised or reinterpreted by local authorities and combines already-established approaches to policing with external approaches to policing. Policing cannot be separated from its political context, as stated in the introduction. Therefore, in order to promote and to establish a community-oriented approach to policing that is in line with the principles of SSR and good governance, a transformative context of democratization is necessary.

Finally, there are definitely prospects for establishing and promoting community policing along the lines of good governance and SSR in developing and transitional countries. However, such endeavours need time, commitment, and resources. It is an enduring and incremental process of harmonizing local professional police organizational capacities with the ideational superstructure of SSR and norms and values inherent in good governance. Simultaneously, there is the challenging but necessary task of creating a local version of community policing that speaks to the local realities and also carries the relevant local ownership.

Recommendations

- **Necessity of existing basic police capacity and knowledge**
  Fostering community policing in developing or transitional countries without the ability to build on a certain level of local bureaucratic and operational police professionalism will not lead to a successful nor a sustained implementation of community policing strategies. The implementation of community policing alone does not help to overcome existing deficiencies within the operational police service and a lack of professional knowledge of policing.
  Community policing is an approach to policing that rests on fundamental basics and the thorough knowledge of policing tools and ethics. Ideally, community policing adds to the already-existing understanding of communication strategies with the communities, of bureaucratic processes, of standard operational procedures, and of laws applicable to the local context. Finally, police professionalism also means accountability on all levels.

Therefore, the implementation of community policing needs to be built on a certain level of police professionalism and bureaucratic capacity. Interlinking capacity building measures with an appropriate normative framework will provide a basis for more sophisticated reform programmes. Unless a certain level of police professionalism is established first, reform initiatives aiming solely at the implementation of community policing will be unrewarding.

- **Necessity of local ownership in adjusting external reform programmes**
Local ownership of police reform is key to ensuring comprehensive and sustained implementation of community policing. Resistance to police reform in general or community policing in particular by the police command as well as the political leadership of a given country may lead to a superficial implementation of community policing elements or even to resistance on behalf of the police officers. These forms of resistance may occur during the presence or after the departure of foreign police trainers and mean the actual failure of the police reform programme.
In some cases, community policing units might still operate to fulfil foreign donors' expectations. However, lining up a rather symbolic unit of community policing is not for the good of the people but rather to maintain the impression of willingness to reform in order to receive continued financial and technical support by foreign donors.
Hence, to avoid these kinds of scenarios, local police leadership and political leaders need to be involved into community policing programming from the start and to contribute to the overall project as much as possible. This close collaboration between foreign and local actors also helps to tailor a country-specific approach to community policing. As the paper's findings suggest, a local reinterpretation of foreign programmes is also necessary to ensure a seamless implementation of a very local approach to policing communities, which is, ideally, in line with principles of SSR and good governance.
However, foreign trainers and programmers should be open to regular alterations and adjustments of their strategies and programmes to meet country-specific developments and obstacles to police reform. Rigid foreign concepts and blueprints on how to promote community policing often proved to be meaningless for a successful and sustained implementation of community policing. This will eventually help to avoid the implementation of one-fits-all community policing strategies, which will become irrelevant not only to the local police but also to the local communities.

- **Integration of local communities and CSO in the reform process**
As police reform requires strong local ownership, local reformers as well as international donors should ensure the inclusion of local communities and civil-society organizations in the reform process. Since police reform in line with SSR principles aims at the establishment of a people-centred, human-security approach to policing, the very recipients of the police service know best what they expect from the police and in which areas they would like to see a change. Ideally, these initiatives should go beyond the common model of police-community fora and provide communities with the possibility for active discussion and shaping the future police service in their country by outlining ideas and concepts. Moreover, integrating community members into committees on strategic development planning of the police will not only facilitate trust in the police organization, but also add to the general feeling that the police are not isolated from but a part of the society. Even after several stages of police reform, community feedback on the police performance is essential to evaluate and to assess reform benchmarks and should therefore maintained.

- **Familiarization of foreign community policing trainers and programmers with the country context**

As several empirical findings on police reform suggest,[243] resorting to ready-made templates for the implementation of community policing in a given country will not bring the anticipated success.

In every country, police-community relationships rest on a local history, evolved traditions, and specific normative perceptions on how to provide security. Moreover, understanding the local context also helps to realize different political agendas and diverging political interests among the local partners. Therefore, external programmes and trainers need to be sensitized with the local context and align their community policing strategies accordingly. Moreover, foreign trainers and programmers should learn to accept local realities and manage their expectations regarding a smooth reform process.

Getting to know the country they are working in not only helps to devise a country-specific community policing programme that speaks to the local realities, but also helps to become accepted by local decision makers and practitioners in the long run.

To conclude, community policing is by far not the only solution to overcome shattered police-community relations. As already mentioned at another point, the performance of the police in a given country reflects the overall political orientation and agenda of the government. For a compelling reason, contemporary SSR follows a comprehensive and all-encompassing agenda: It not only focuses on single institutions or actors but aims at the reform of the whole political system and, ideally, at affiliated agencies and organizations as well. Therefore, focussing solely on the implementation of a vaguely formulated community policing approach and ticking boxes on default best-practice indicators in a country where police brutality and impunity prevail will not foster sustained change.

Community policing can and should be *one* element of international development cooperation as part of SSR as far as the local preconditions of a professionally developed policing body and the necessary local political commitment to reform are given. Promoting community-oriented approaches to policing in these favourable contexts, however, also means departing from Western best-practice standards and assisting local actors in the formulation of applicable and relevant local approaches to pluralist and rule of law-based policing.

Notes

1 United Nations Security Council (2014): The Maintenance of International Peace and Security: Security Sector Reform: Challenges and Opportunities, S/RES/2151 (2014); 28 April 2014. New York: United Nations, United Nations Security Council (2014): S/RES/2185 (2014); 20 November 2014. New York: United Nations.

2 See, for instance, United Nations Security Council (2000): Report of the Secretary-General on the United Nations Transitional Administration in East Timor, S/2000/738; 26 July 2000. New York: United Nations, United Nations Security Council (2002): Report of the Secretary-General on the United Nations Transitional Administration in East Timor, S/2002/432; 17 April 2002. New York: United Nations.

3 See more in Mike Brogden (2005): "Horses for Courses" and "Thin Blue Lines": Community policing in transitional society. In: Police Quarterly, 8 (1), 64–98; Dominique Wisler and Ihekwoaba D. Onwudiwe (2008): Community policing in comparison. In: Police Quarterly, 11 (4), 427–446; Helene Maria Kyed (2009): Community policing in post-war Mozambique. In: Policing and Society, 19 (4), 354–371; Alice Hills (2008): The dialectic of police reform in Nigeria. In: The Journal of Modern African Studies, 46 (2), 215–234. See also, on the transformation of the South African Police (SAP) to the South African Police Service (SAPS) and its initially much-lauded transformation towards community-oriented policing: Steffen Jensen (2014): Conflicting Logics of Exceptionality: New Beginnings and the Problem of Police Violence in Post-Apartheid South Africa. In: Development and Change, 45 (3), 458–478; Monique Marks (2005): Transforming the robocops; Changing police in South Africa. Scottsville: University of KwaZulu-Natal Press; Jonny Steinberg (2011): Crime prevention goes abroad: Policy transfer and policing in post-apartheid South Africa. In: Theoretical Criminology, 15 (4), 349–364; Jonny Steinberg (2012): Establishing Police Authority and Civilian Compliance in Post-Apartheid Johannesburg: An Argument from the Work of Egon Bittner. In: Policing and Society, 22 (4), 481–495; Anthony Altbeker (2009): The Building of the New South African Police Service; The Dynamics of Police Reform in a Changing (and Violent) Country. In: Mercedes S. Hinton and Tim Newburn (eds.): Policing Developing Democracies. New York: Routledge. 260–279; Jonny Steinberg (2012): Security and disappointment: Policing, freedom and xenophobia in South Africa. In: British Journal of Criminology, 52, 345–360.

[4] Charles Tilly (2006): Why and how history matters. In: Robert E. Goodin and Charles Tilly (eds.): The Oxford handbook of contextual political analysis. Oxford: Oxford University Press. 417–437; James Mahoney and Daniel Schensul (2006): Historical context and path dependence. In: Robert E. Goodin and Charles Tilly (eds.): The Oxford handbook of contextual political analysis. Oxford: Oxford University Press. 454–471; James Mahoney and Dietrich Rueschemeyer (eds.) (2003): Comparative historical analysis in the social sciences. Cambridge: Cambridge University Press.

[5] Robert Egnell and Peter Haldén (2009): Laudable, Ahistorical and Overambitious: Security Sector Reform Meets State Formation Theory. In: Conflict, Security & Development, 9 (1), 27–54.

[6] John Alderson (1979): Policing Freedom: A Commentary on the Dilemmas of Policing in Western Democracies. Plymouth: Macdonald and Evans, John Alderson (1983): Community policing, The future of policing – Papers presented to 15th Cropwood Round-Table Conference, Cropwood Conference Series No. 15. Cambridge: University of Cambridge.

[7] Herman Goldstein (1990): Problem-oriented policing. Philadelphia: Temple University Press.

[8] Organisation for Economic Co-operation and Development (2007): OECD-DAC handbook on security system reform: Supporting security and justice. Paris: OECD.

[9] Organisation for Economic Co-operation and Development (2007): OECD-DAC handbook on security system reform: Supporting security and justice: 21f.

[10] United Nations Security Council (2014): The Maintenance of International Peace and Security: Security Sector Reform: Challenges and Opportunities, S/RES/2151 (2014); 28 April 2014.

[11] Edward Newman, Roland Paris and Oliver P. Richmond (2009): Introduction. In: Edward Newman, Roland Paris and Oliver P. Richmond (eds.): New perspectives on liberal peacebuilding. Tokyo: United Nations University Press. 3–25; Bethan K. Greener (2012): Popperian statebuilding, policing and the Liberal Peace. In: Journal of Intervention and Statebuilding, 6 (4), 407–426; Nicole Ball (2010): The evolution of the security sector reform agenda. In: Mark Sedra (ed.): The future of Security Sector Reform. Waterloo: Centre for International Governance (CIGI). 29–44.

[12] Albrecht Schnabel (2009): Ideal requirements versus real environments in security sector reform. In: Hans Born and Albrecht Schnabel (eds.): Security sector reform in challenging environments. Münster: Lit. 3–36: 7; Fairlie Chappuis (2011): Human security and security sector reform: Conceptual convergences in theory and practice. In: Wolfgang Benedek, Matthias C. Kettemann and Markus Möstl (eds.): Mainstreaming human security in peace operations and crisis management: Policies, problems, potential. London: Routledge. 99–122: 102; Organisation for Economic Co-operation and Development (2007): OECD-DAC handbook on security system reform; Supporting security and justice: 112ff.

[13] Organisation for Economic Co-operation and Development (2007): OECD-DAC handbook on security system reform; Supporting security and justice: 163f.

[14] Chappuis (2011): Human security and security sector reform; Conceptual convergences in theory and practice: 103f.

[15] See, among others, Thomas C. Bruneau (2005): The militaries in post-conflict societies: Lessons from Central America and prospects for Colombia. In: Albrecht Schnabel and Hans-Georg Ehrhart (eds.): Security sector reform and post-conflict peacebuilding. Tokyo: United Nations University Press. 225–242; Donald Stoker (2008): The history and evolution of foreign military advising and assistance, 1815–2007. In: Donald Stoker (ed.): Military advising and assistance; From mercenaries to privatization, 1815–2007. Abingdon: Routledge. 1–10; John Samuel Fitch (1979): The political impact of U.S. military aid to Latin America: Institutional and individual effects. In: Armed Forces & Society, 5, 360–386; Stathis N. Kalyvas and Laia Balcells (2010): International system and technologies of rebellion: How the end of the Cold War shaped internal conflict. In: The American Political Science Review, 104 (3), 415–429.

[16] On the negative outcomes of one-sided training support, see Carl Forsberg and Tim Sullivan (2016): Criminal patronage networks and the struggle to rebuild the Afghan state. In: Michelle Hughes and Michael Miklaucic (eds.): Impunity: Countering illicit power in war and transition. Washington, D.C.: National Defense University. 12–39: 22–26. On the necessity to interlink technical assistance with institutional reform, see also Jeffrey Isima (2010): Scaling the hurdle or muddling through coordination and sequencing implementation of security sector reform in Africa. In: Mark Sedra (ed.): The future of security sector reform. Waterloo: Centre for International Governance Innovation (CIGI). 327–338.

[17] See Gary W. Cordner and Kathryn E. Scarborough (2010): Police administration. New Providence: LexisNexis, Deborah Eade et al. (1995): Capacity building for development. In: Deborah Eade and Suzanne Williams (eds.): The Oxfam handbook of development and relief. Oxford: Oxfam. 395–473.

[18] Hans Born (2009): Security sector reform in challenging environments: Insights from comparative analysis. In: Hans Born and Albrecht Schnabel (eds.): Security sector reform in challenging environments. Münster: Lit. 241–266: 257.

[19] Peter Albrecht, Finn Stepputat and Louise Andersen (2010): Security sector reform, the European way. In: Mark Sedra (ed.): The future of security sector reform. Waterloo: Centre for International Governance (CIGI). 74–87: 84f; Mark Sedra (2010): Towards second generation security sector reform. In: Mark Sedra (ed.): The future of security sector reform. Waterloo: Centre for International Governance Innovation (CIGI). 102–116: 102–204.

[20] Alpaslan Özerdem and Sung Yong Lee (2015): Introduction. In: Sung Yong Lee and Alpaslan Özerdem (eds.): Local ownership in international peacekeeping: Key theoretical and practical issues. London: Routledge. 1–16; Fairlie Chappuis and Heiner Hänggi (2013): Statebuilding through security sector reform. In: David Chandler and Timothy D. Sisk (eds.): Handbook of international statebuilding. London: Routledge. 168–184: 178.

[21] United Nations Security Council (2014): The Maintenance of International Peace and Security: Security Sector Reform: Challenges and Opportunities, S/RES/2151 (2014); 28 April 2014, United Nations Security Council (2014): S/RES/2185 (2014); 20 November 2014.

[22] Laurie Nathan (2008): The challenge of local ownership of SSR: From donor rhetoric to practice. In: Timothy Donais (ed.): Local ownership and security sector reform. Münster: Lit. 19–36: 20f; Alan Bryden (2004): Understanding security sector reform and reconstruction. In: Alan Bryden and Heiner Hänggi (eds.): Reform and reconstruction of the security sector. Münster: Lit. 259–275: 268; Timothy Donais (2008): Understanding local ownership in security sector reform. In: Timothy Donais (ed.): Local ownership and security sector reform. Münster: Lit. 3–17: 3.

[23] Timothy Donais (2015): Ownership: From policy to practice. In: Paul Jackson (ed.): Handbook of international security and development. Cheltenham: Edward Elgar. 227–247: 227.

[24] Hideaki Shinoda (2015): Local ownership as a strategic guideline for peacebuilding. In: Sung Yong Lee and Alpaslan Özerdem (eds.): Local ownership in international peacekeeping: Key theoretical and practical issues. London: Routledge. 19–38: 32f; Antoine Rayroux and Nina Wilén (2014): Resisting ownership: The paralysis of EU peacebuilding in the Congo. In: African Security, 7 (1), 24–44.

[25] Sung Yong Lee and Alpaslan Özerdem (2015): Conclusion. In: Sung Yong Lee and Alpaslan Özerdem (eds.): Local ownership in international peacekeeping: Key theoretical and practical issues. London: Routledge. 195–207: 196–199.

[26] Donais (2015): Ownership: From policy to practice: 229; Peter Albrecht (2015): Building on what works: Local actors and service delivery in fragile situations. In: Paul Jackson (ed.): Handbook of international security and development. Cheltenham: Edward Elgar. 279–293: 281.

[27] Thomas Muehlmann (2008): Police restructuring in Bosnia-Herzegovina: Problems of internationally-led security sector reform. In: Journal of Intervention and Statebuilding, 2 (1), 1–22: 3.

[28] For similar cases, see Brogden (2005): "Horses for Courses" and "Thin Blue Lines": Community policing in transitional society; Giovanna Bono (2013): EU police missions. In: David Chandler and Timothy D. Sisk (eds.): Handbook of international statebuilding. London: Routledge. 350–361: 355; Deniz Kocak (2016): Security Sector Reconstruction in Post-Conflict: The Lessons from Timor-Leste. In: Michelle Hughes and Michael Miklaucic (eds.): Impunity: Countering Illicit Power in War and Transition. Washington, D.C.: National Defense University. 348–365.

[29] Donais (2015): Ownership: From policy to practice: 230–232; Donais (2008): Operationalising local ownership in SSR: 277.

[30] Albrecht (2015): Building on what works: Local actors and service delivery in fragile situations: 288.

[31] On the centrality of the police, see Mark Neocleous (2000): The fabrication of social order: A critical theory of police power. London: Pluto Press; and Robert Reiner (2000): The Politics of the Police. Oxford: Oxford University Press.

[32] Michael Lipson (2007): A "garbage can model" of UN Peacekeeping. In: Global Governance, 13, 79–97; Barry J. Ryan (2011): Statebuilding and Police Reform: The Freedom of Security. London: Routledge; Philipp Rotmann (2011): First steps towards a police doctrine for UN peace operations (2001–2006). In: Policing and Society: An International Journal of Research and Policy, 21 (1), 84–95; Halvor Hartz (2000): CIVPOL: The UN instrument for police reform. In: Tor Tanke Holm and Espen Barth Eide (eds.): Peacebuilding and police reform. London: Frank Cass Publishers. 27–42.

[33] See Mary Kaldor (1999): New and old wars: Organized violence in a global era. Stanford: Stanford University Press; see also John Rapley (2006): The new middle ages. In: Foreign Affairs, 85 (3), 95–103; Mary Kaldor (2013): In defence of new wars. In: Stability: International Journal of Security & Development, 2 (4), 1–16.

[34] See United Nations General Assembly (2000): Report of the Panel on United Nations Peace Operations, A/55/305, 21 August 2000. New York: United Nations; United Nations General Assembly (1992): A/RES/47/120; 18 December 1992; Charles T. Hunt (2015): UN peace operations and international policing: Negotiating complexity, assessing impact and learning to learn. London: Routledge: 28f.

[35] David H. Bayley and Robert M. Perito (2010): The Police in War: Fighting Insurgency, Terrorism, and Violent Crime. Boulder: Lynne Rienner Publishers; Peter H. Gantz (2007): The postconflict security gap and the United Nations peace operations system. In: Muna Ndulo (ed.): Security, reconstruction, and reconciliation: When the wars end. London: UCL Press. 247–275.

[36] Chuck Call and Michael Barnett (2000): Looking for a few good cops: Peacekeeping, peacebuilding and CIVPOL. In: Tor Tanke Holm and Espen Barth Eide (eds.): Peacebuilding and police reform. London: Frank Cass Publishers. 43–68: 47.

[37] Timothy Edmunds (2006): What are armed forces for? The changing nature of military roles in Europe. In: International Affairs, 82 (6), 1059–1075: 1070.

[38] See United Nations General Assembly (2000): Report of the Panel on United Nations Peace Operations, A/55/305, 21 August 2000: para 39,118; Bethan K. Greener (2011): The rise of policing in peace operations. In: International Peacekeeping, 18 (2), 183–195.

[39] Ryan (2011): Statebuilding and Police Reform: The Freedom of Security: 72–75; Annika S. Hansen (2002): From Congo to Kosovo: Civilian police in peace operations, Adelphi Paper 343. London: International Institute for Strategic Studies (IISS). 21; United Nations (2000): United Nations Civilian Police principles and guidelines. New York: United Nations Department for Peacekeeping Operations.

[40] See the UNSC resolutions on Bosnia and Herzegovina: United Nations Security Council (1996): S/RES/1088 (1996); 12 December 1996, Liberia: United Nations Security Council (2003): S/RES/1509 (2003); 19 September 2003; and Sudan: United Nations Security Council (2006): S/RES/1706 (2006); 31 August 2006.

[41] Mike Brogden and Preeti Nijhar (2005): Community Policing: National and International Models and Approaches. Devon: Willan Publishing: 233; Ursula C. Schroeder, Fairlie Chappuis, and Deniz Kocak (2014): Security Sector Reform and the Emergence of Hybrid Security Governance. In: International Peacekeeping, 12 (2), 214–230: 224f; Lisa Denney and Sarah Jenkins (2013): Securing communities: The what and how of community policing, ODI Background Paper. London: Overseas Development Institute. 9.

[42] United Nations Security Council (2014): S/RES/2185 (2014); 20 November 2014; United Nations Security Council (2014): The Maintenance of International Peace and Security: Security Sector Reform: Challenges and Opportunities, S/RES/2151 (2014); 28 April 2014.

[43] For a thorough discussion on the Peelian Metropolitan Policing approach see the chapter "Origins of Community Policing".

[44] David H. Bayley (2006): Changing the guard: Developing democratic police abroad. New York: Oxford University Press: 62.

[45] Bayley (2006): Changing the guard: Developing democratic police abroad: 19; Nathan W. Pino and Michael D. Wiatrowski (2006): The principles of democratic policing. In: Nathan W. Pino and Michael D. Wiatrowski (eds.): Democratic policing in transitional and developing countries. Aldershot: Ashgate. 69–97: 83.

[46] Charles T. Call (2007): Introduction: What we know and don't know about postconflict justice and security reform. In: Charles T. Call (ed.): Constructing justice and security after war. Washington, D.C.: United States Institute of Peace Press. 3–26: 6f; Bayley (2006): Changing the guard: Developing democratic police abroad: 19f.

[47] Bayley (2006): Changing the guard: Developing democratic police abroad: 20; David H. Bayley (2001): Democratizing the police abroad: What to do and how to do it. Washington, D.C.: U.S. National Institute of Justice, Department of Justice. 14f.

[48] Michael D. Wiatrowski and Jack A. Goldstone (2010): The ballot and the badge: Democratic policing. In: Journal of Democracy, 21 (2), 79–92: 81; Bayley and Perito (2010): The Police in War: Fighting Insurgency, Terrorism, and Violent-Crime: 84–86.

[49] Pino and Wiatrowski (2006): The principles of democratic policing: 71, 81; see, among others, Organisation for Security and Co-operation in Europe (2008): Guidebook on democratic policing by the Senior Police Advisor to the OSCE Secretary General. Vienna: OSCE.

[50] David Alan Sklansky (2008): Democracy and the police. Stanford: Stanford University Press: 189–191.

[51] See Alice Hills (2009): The possibility of transnational policing. In: Policing and Society, 19 (3), 300–317: 304; Brogden and Nijhar (2005): Community Policing: National and International Models and Approaches: 4f; Schroeder, Chappuis, and Kocak (2014): Security Sector Reform and the Emergence of Hybrid Security Governance: 215, 224f.

[52] Organisation for Security and Co-operation in Europe (2008): Guidebook on democratic policing by the Senior Police Advisor to the OSCE Secretary General: 28.

[53] Organisation for Security and Co-operation in Europe (2008): Good practices in building police-public partnerships by the Senior Police Advisor to the OSCE Secretary General. Vienna: OSCE: 20.

[54] See Bayley and Perito (2010): The Police in War: Fighting Insurgency, Terrorism, and Violent Crime: 86; David H. Bayley (2005): Police reform as foreign policy. In: The Australian and New Zealand Journal of Criminology, 38 (2), 206–215: 208.

[55] Bayley and Perito (2010): The Police in War: Fighting Insurgency, Terrorism, and Violent Crime: 3, 83f.

[56] Bayley and Perito (2010): The Police in War: Fighting Insurgency, Terrorism, and Violent Crime: 83–86.

[57] Bayley and Perito (2010): The Police in War: Fighting Insurgency, Terrorism, and Violent Crime: 86f.

[58] Sybille De La Rosa (2008): Aneignung oder Annäherung. Zwei Formen interkultureller Kommunikation. In: Sybille De La Rosa, Ulrike Höppner, and Matthias Kötter (eds.): Transdisziplinäre Governanceforschung; Gemeinsam hinter den Staat blicken. Baden-Baden: Nomos. 80–99: 81.

[59] See Georgina Sinclair (2006): At the end of the line: Colonial policing and the imperial endgame 1945–80. Manchester: Manchester University Press: 16f.

[60] Martin Thomas (2012): Violence and colonial order. Cambridge: Cambridge University Press: 6, 18.

[61] Stefan Rinke, Mónika Contreras Saiz, and Lasse Hölck (2012): Appropriation and resistance mechanisms in (post-)colonial constellations of actors: The Latin American frontiers in the 18th and 19th century, SFB-Governance Working Paper Series, No. 30. Berlin: Collaborative Research Center (SFB) 700. 5.

[62] Ben Crewe (2007): Power, adaptation and resistance in a late-modern men's prison. In: British Journal of Criminology, 47, 256–275.

[63] Crewe (2007): Power, adaptation and resistance in a late-modern men's prison: 257, 273.

[64] Niels Uildriks and Piet van Reenen (2003): Policing post-communist societies: Police-public violence, democratic policing and human rights. Antwerp: Intersentia; Antoine Vandemoortele (2012): Adaptation, resistance and a (re)turn to functionalism: The case of the Bosnian police restructuring process (2003–2008). In: European Security, 21 (2), 202–218.

[65] Uildriks and van Reenen (2003): Policing post-communist societies: Police-public violence, democratic policing and human rights: 28–30.

[66] The conceptual framework of this paper builds on an earlier strand of research by the Collaborative Research Centre (SFB) 700 "Governance in Areas of Limited Statehood", which conducted comprehensive cross-disciplinary research on governance transfers.

[67] Anke Draude (2012): Die Vielfalt des Regierens: Eine Governance-Konzeption jenseits des Eurozentrismus. Frankfurt/Main: Campus-Verlag: 236; Rinke, Contreras Saiz, and Hölck (2012): Appropriation and resistance mechanisms in (post-)colonial constellations of actors: The Latin American frontiers in the 18th and 19th century, SFB-Governance Working Paper Series, No. 30. Berlin: Collaborative Research Center (SFB) 700: 6; see also Thomas R. Eimer (2012): When modern science meets traditional knowledge: A multi-level process of adaptation and resistance, SFB-Governance Working Paper Series, No. 35. Berlin: Collaborative Research Center (SFB) 700.

[68] De La Rosa (2008): Aneignung oder Annäherung. Zwei Formen interkultureller Kommunikation: 86; Johannes Paulmann (1998): Interkultureller Transfer zwischen Deutschland und Großbritannien: Einführung in ein Forschungskonzept. In: Rudolf Muhs, Johannes Paulmann, and Willibald Steinmetz (eds.): Aneignung und Abwehr; Interkultureller Transfer zwischen Deutschland und Großbritannien im 19. Jahrhundert. Bodenheim: Philo. 21–43: 25, 33; Draude (2012): Die Vielfalt des Regierens: Eine Governance-Konzeption jenseits des Eurozentrismus: 236f.

[69] Jack S. Levy (2007): Qualitative methods and cross-method dialogue in political science. In: Comparative Political Studies, 40 (2), 196–214: 209; James Mahoney (2000): Strategies of causal inference in small-N analysis. In: Sociological Methods & Research, 28 (4), 387–424; James Mahoney (1999): Nominal, ordinal, and narrative appraisal in macrocausal analysis. In: American Journal of Sociology, 104 (4), 1154–1196; David J. Harding and Krisitn S. Seefeldt (2013): Mixed methods and casual analysis. In: Stephen L. Morgan (ed.): Handbook of causal analysis for social research. Dordrecht: Springer. 91–110: 93f.

[70] David H. Bayley and Clifford D. Shearing (1996): The future of policing. In: Law & Society Review, 30 (3), 585–606: 588.

[71] Melissa Schaefer Morabito (2010): Understanding community policing as an innovation: Patterns of adoption. In: Crime & Delinquency, 56 (4), 564–587: 564f; Jerome H. Skolnick and David H. Bayley (1988): Theme and variation in community policing. In: Crime and Justice, 10: 1–37: 3; Alderson (1979): Policing Freedom: A Commentary on the Dilemmas of Policing in Western Democracies: 38–42.

[72] Wesley G. Skogan (2006): The promise of community policing. In: David Weisburd and Anthony A. Braga (eds.): Police innovation: Contrasting perspectives. Cambridge: Cambridge University Press. 27–43: 28–31; Schaefer Morabito (2010): Understanding community policing as an innovation: Patterns of adoption: 565; Alistair Henry (2007): Policing and ethnic minorities. In: Alistair Henry and David J. Smith (eds.): Transformations of policing. Aldershot: Ashgate. 79–111: 81.

[73] The listed principles are an excerpt out of Alderson's ten original principles: Alderson (1979): Policing Freedom: A Commentary on the Dilemmas of Policing in Western Democracies: 199.

[74] Alderson (1979): Policing Freedom: A Commentary on the Dilemmas of Policing in Western Democracies: 200f.

[75] Alderson (1983): Community policing: The future of policing – Papers presented to 15th Cropwood Round-Table Conference, Cropwood Conference Series No. 15. Cambridge: University of Cambridge; Ian Loader and Neil Walker (2001): Policing as public good: Reconstituting the connections between policing and the state. In: Theoretical Criminology, 5 (1), 9–35: 25; Peter Hough (2013): Understanding global security. London: Routledge: 9f; Ball (2010): The evolution of the security sector reform agenda: 32.

[76] Leslie G. Scarman (1981): The Scarman report: Report of an inquiry by the Right Honourable the Lord Scarman. Harmondsworth: Penguin Books.

[77] Scarman (1981): The Scarman report: Report of an inquiry by the Right Honourable the Lord Scarman: 200f.

[78] Alderson (1983): Community policing: The future of policing – Papers presented to 15th Cropwood Round-Table Conference, Cropwood Conference Series No. 15. Cambridge: University of Cambridge.

[79] Kenneth Newman (1984): Report for the Commissioner of the Metropolis 1983. London: Her Majesty's Stationery Office: 8.

[80] Benjamin Bowling (1998): Violent racism: Victimization, policing and social context. Oxford: Clarendon Press: 298.

[81] Reiner (2000): The Politics of the Police: 110f; Tim Newburn (2003): Policing since 1945. In: Tim Newburn (ed.): Handbook of policing. Devon: Willan Publishing. 84–105: 86f.

[82] Brogden (2005): "Horses for Courses" and "Thin Blue Lines": Community policing in transitional society: 74.

[83] Skogan (2006): The promise of community policing: 27.

[84] David L. Carter (1999): A response to "Community policing: Thriving because it works". In: Police Quarterly, 2 (1), 103–109: 106–108; Peter K. Manning (1997): Police work: The social organization of policing. Prospect Heights: Waveland Press: 15.

[85] Stephen Mastrofski (2006): Community policing: A skeptical view. In: David Weisburd and Anthony A. Braga (eds.): Police innovation; Contrasting perspectives. Cambridge: Cambridge University Press. 44–73: 47f.

[86] Schaefer Morabito (2010): Understanding community policing as an innovation: Patterns of adoption: 565; Carter (1999): A response to "Community policing: Thriving because it works": 106–108; Dennis P. Rosenbaum, Sandy Yeh, and Deanna L. Wilkinson (1994): Impact of community policing on police personnel: A quasi-experimental test. In: Crime & Delinquency, 40 (3), 331–353: 332.

[87] Jennifer Brown (2007): From cult of masculinity to smart macho: Gender perspectives on police occupational culture. In: Megan O'Neill, Monique Marks, and Anne-Marie Singh (eds.): Police occupational culture: New debates and directions. Oxford: Elsevier. 205–226: 206f, 216f; John Van Maanen (1974): Working the street: A developmental view of police behavior. In: Herbert Jacob (ed.): The potential for reform of criminal justice. Beverly Hills: SAGE Publications. 83–130: 87f, 105; Bethan Loftus (2009): Police culture in a changing world. Oxford: Oxford University Press: 96–99.

[88] See Janet Chan (1997): Changing police culture: Policing a multicultural society. Cambridge: Cambridge University Press; Loftus (2009): Police culture in a changing world; John P. Crank (1998): Understanding police culture. Cincinnati: Anderson Publishing; Peter K. Manning (2007): A dialectic of organisational and occupational culture. In: Megan O'Neill, Monique Marks, and Anne-Marie Singh (eds.): Police occupational culture: New debates and directions. Oxford: Elsevier. 47–83; Tom Cockcroft (2013): Police culture: Themes and concepts. London: Routledge; David J. MacCarthy (2013): Gendering 'soft' policing: Multi-agency working, female cops, and the fluidities of police culture/s. In: Policing and Society, 23 (2), 261–278.

[89] William A. Westley (1970): Violence and the police: A sociological study of law, custom, and morality. Cambridge: The MIT Press: 10; see also Reiner (2000): The Politics of the Police: 86; Andrew Goldsmith (1990): Taking police culture seriously: Police discretion and the limits of law. In: Policing and Society, 1 (2), 91–114; Tim Prenzler (1997): Is there a police culture? In: Australian Journal of Public Administration, 56 (4), 47–56.

[90] Mastrofski (2006): Community policing: A skeptical view: 47; Skogan (2006): The promise of community policing: 27.

[91] See Marleen Easton and Paul Ponsaers (2010): The view of the police on community policing in Belgian multicultural neighbourhoods. In: Marc Cools, Brice De Ruyver, Marleen Easton, Lieven Pauwels, Paul Ponsaers, Gudrun Vande Walle, Tom Vander Beken, Freya Vander Laenen, Gert Vermeulen, and Gerwinde Vynckier (eds.): Safety, societal problems and citizen's perceptions: New empirical data, theories and analyses. Antwerpen: Maklu. 161–182: 173f.

[92] See Marianne Bevan and Megan H. MacKenzie (2012): 'Cowboy' Policing versus 'the Softer Stuff'. In: International Feminist Journal of Politics, 14 (4), 508–528.

[93] See Arthur J. Lurigio and Wesley G. Skogan (1994): Winning the hearts and minds of police officers: An assessment of staff perceptions of community policing in Chicago. In: Crime & Delinquency, 40 (3), 315–330: 315f; Loftus (2009): Police culture in a changing world: 13f.

[94] See, among others, Brogden and Nijhar (2005): Community Policing: National and International Models and Approaches; Piet van Reenen (2014): The rule of law, human rights and changing the police in some Latin American countries. In: J. L. Hovens (ed.): Building police integrity: A post-conflict perspective. The Hague: Royal Netherlands Marechaussee. 297–340: 307; Victor E. Kappeler and Peter B. Kraska (2015): Normalising police militarisation, living in denial. In: Policing and Society, 25 (3), 268–275: 275; Victor E. Kappeler and Larry K. Gaines (2011): Community policing; A contemporary perspective. London: Routledge: 6f; William Lyons (2007): A critique of community policing. In: Klaus Mladek (ed.): Police forces: A cultural history of an institution. Houndmills: Palgrave Macmillan. 199–220.

[95] Lyons (2007): A critique of community policing: 212; see also Pino and Wiatrowski (2006): Policing and police reform in the US: Adequate for export?: 65; Sklansky (2008): Democracy and the police: 116.

[96] Lyons (2007): A critique of community policing: 201f; William Lyons (1999): The politics of community policing: Rearranging the power to punish. Ann Arbor: University of Michigan Press.

[97] Adam Crawford and Karen Evans (2012): Crime prevention and community safety. In: Mike Maguire, Rod Morgan and Robert Reiner (eds.): The Oxford handbook of criminology. Oxford: Oxford University Press. 769–805: 787.

[98] Bill Dixon (2004): Community policing: "Cherry pie" or melktert? In: Society in Transition, 35 (2), 251–272: 254.

[99] Peter B. Kraska (2007): Militarization and policing – Its relevance to 21st century police. In: Policing, 1 (4), 501–513: 507; Matthew T. DeMichele and Peter B. Kraska (2001): Community policing in battle garb: A paradox or coherent strategy? In: Peter B. Kraska (ed.): Militarizing the American criminal justice system: The changing roles of the armed forces and the police. Boston: Northeastern University Press. 82–101: 95; Kappeler and Kraska (2015): Normalising police militarisation, living in denial: 275; but see also Garth den Heyer (2014): Mayberry revisited: A review of the influence of police paramilitary units on policing. In: Policing and Society, 24 (3), 346–361.

[100] James Q. Wilson and George L. Kelling (1982): Broken windows. In: The Atlantic, 249 (2), 29–38.

[101] Wilson and Kelling (1982): Broken windows: 31f; George L. Kelling and Catherine M. Coles (1997): Fixing broken windows; Restoring order and reducing crime in our communities. New York: Touchstone: 19f.

[102] Wilson and Kelling (1982): Broken windows: 29–31.

[103] Kelling and Coles (1997): Fixing broken windows: Restoring order and reducing crime in our communities: 96–98.

[104] Ralph B. Taylor (2006): Incivilities reduction policing, zero tolerance, and the retreat from coproduction: Weak foundations and strong pressures. In: David Weisburd and Anthony A. Braga (eds.): Police innovation: Contrasting perspectives. Cambridge: Cambridge University Press. 98–114: 103; William H. Sousa and George L. Kelling (2006): Of "broken windows", criminology, and criminal justice. In: David Weisburd and Anthony A. Braga (eds.): Police innovation: Contrasting perspectives. Cambridge: Cambridge University Press. 77–97: 83–85.

[105] Lucia Zedner (2003): Too much security. In: International Journal of the Sociology of Law, 31, 155–184: 175; DeMichele and Kraska (2001): Community policing in battle garb: A paradox or coherent strategy?: 86f.

[106] Roger Hopkins Burke (2012): Criminal justice theory: An introduction. London: Routledge: 12; Roger Hopkins Burke (1998): A contextualisation of zero tolerance policing strategies. In: Roger Hopkins Burke (ed.): Zero tolerance policing. Leicester: Perpetuity Press. 11–38: 16; Burke (1998): A contextualisation of zero tolerance policing strategies.

[107] Burke (1998): A contextualisation of zero tolerance policing strategies: 12, 21.

[108] Pierre Aepli, Olivier Ribaux and Everett Summerfield (2011): Decision making in policing; Operations and management. Lausanne: EPFL Press: 104.

[109] Cynthia Lum (2009): Community policing or zero tolerance? Preferences of police officers from 22 countries in transition. In: British Journal of Criminology, 49, 788–809: 794.

[110] Bob Knights (1998): The "Slide to Ashes": An antidote to zero tolerance. In: Roger Hopkins Burke (ed.): Zero tolerance policing. Leicester: Perpetuity Press. 91–103: 91.

[111] Taylor (2006): Incivilities reduction policing, zero tolerance, and the retreat from coproduction: Weak foundations and strong pressures: 107f.

[112] Goldstein (1990): Problem-oriented policing.

[113] Goldstein (1990): Problem-oriented policing: 32f.

[114] John E. Eck (2006): Science, values, and problem-oriented policing: Why problem-oriented policing? In: David Weisburd and Anthony A. Braga (eds.): Police innovation; Contrasting perspectives. Cambridge: Cambridge University Press. 117–132: 121; Tim Newburn

and Robert Reiner (2012): Policing and the police. In: Mike Maguire, Rod Morgan and Robert Reiner (eds.): The Oxford handbook of criminology. Oxford: Oxford University Press. 806–837: 820f.

[115] Aepli, Ribaux, and Summerfield (2011): Decision making in policing: Operations and management: 104.

[116] Anthony A. Braga and David Weisburd (2006): Problem-oriented policing: The disconnect between principles and practice. In: David Weisburd and Anthony A. Braga (eds.): Police innovation: Contrasting perspectives. Cambridge: Cambridge University Press. 133–152: 145f.

[117] Sklansky (2008): Democracy and the police: 121f.

[118] Braga and Weisburd (2006): Problem-oriented policing: The disconnect between principles and practice: 134–141.

[119] See Carter (1999): A response to "Community policing: Thriving because it works"; Dilip K. Das and Arvind Verma (2003): Police Mission: Challenges and Responses. Lanham: Scarecrow Press; Brogden and Nijhar (2005): Community Policing: National and International Models and Approaches; Roger Hopkins Burke (2004): Introduction: Policing contemporary society. In: Roger Hopkings Burke (ed.): Hard cop, soft cop: Dilemmas and debates in contemporary policing. Devon: Willan Publishing. 1–22.

[120] Das and Verma (2003): Police Mission: Challenges and Responses, Sinclair Dinnen, and John Braithwaite (2009): Reinventing policing through the prism of the colonial kiap. In: Policing and Society, 19 (2), 161–173; Susan A. Lentz and Robert H. Chaires (2007): The invention of Peel's principles: A study of policing 'textbook' history. In: Journal of Criminal Justice, 35, 69–79: 70.

[121] See more in Norman Gash (1979): Aristocracy and people: Britain 1815–1865: The new history of England 8. London: Edward Arnold, Edgar J. Feuchtwanger (1985): Democracy and empire: Britain 1865–1914: The new history of England 9. London: Edward Arnold.

[122] Das and Verma (2003): Police Mission: Challenges and Responses: 7.

[123] Clive Emsley (1996): Crime and society in England, 1750-1900. London: Longman: 216–219; Dominik Nagl (2013): No part of the mother country, but distinct dominions: Rechtstransfer, Staatsbildung und Governance in England, Massachusetts und South Carolina, 1630–1769. Münster: Lit: 129f, 140f.

[124] Pamela D. Mayhall (1979): Police-community relations and the administration of justice. New York: John Wiley & Sons: 6f; Lentz and Chaires (2007): The invention of Peel's principles: A study of policing 'textbook' history: 72f; Clive Emsley (2014): Peel's Principles, Police Principles. In: Jennifer M. Brown (ed.): The Future of Policing. Abingdon: Routledge. 11–22: 13f.

[125] Emsley (2014:11f) as well as Lentz and Chaires (2007:73f) argue that Peel's principles are not grounded on primary materials by Peel but are based on secondary sources by several historians during the 20th century, such as Charles Reith (1952) and Melville Lee (1901). In fact, Emsley (2014:20) even describes Peel's traded principles as a "mythical model" since much of the principles appears to be rather a zeitgeist interpretation of what *good* policing should entail.

[126] Jerome H. Skolnick and James J. Fyfe (1993): Above the law: Police and the excessive use of force. New York: The Free Press: 70f; Emsley (2014): Peel's Principles, Police Principles: 15.

[127] Emsley (1996): Crime and society in England, 1750–1900: 21; Clive Emsley (1996): The English police: A political and social history. London: Longman: 222f.

[128] Eric H. Monkkonen (1992): History of urban police. In: Michael Tonry and Norval Morris (eds.): Modern policing. Chicago: University of Chicago Press. 547–580: 551.

[129] James H. Auten (1981): The paramilitary model of police and police professionalism. In: Police Studies, 4 (2), 67–78: 67; Egon Bittner (1970): The functions of the police in modern society:

A review of background factors, current practices, and possible role models. Chevy Chase: National Institute of Mental Health: 52f; Skolnick and Fyfe (1993): Above the law: Police and the excessive use of force: 117; Emsley (2014): Peel's Principles, Police Principles: 15.

[130] Emsley (2014): Peel's Principles, Police Principles: 15.

[131] Clive Emsley (2003): The Birth and Development of the Police. In: Tim Newburn (ed.): Handbook of Policing. Devon: Willan Publishing. 66–83: 68f.

[132] Emsley (1996): Crime and society in England, 1750–1900: 226–233.

[133] Brogden and Nijhar (2005): Community Policing: National and International Models and Approaches: 172.

[134] Tom Ellis, Chris Lewis, Koichi Hamai, and Tom Williamson (2008): Japanese community policing under the microscope. In: Tom Williamson (ed.): The handbook of knowledge-based policing: Current conceptions and future directions. Chichester: John Wiley & Sons. 157–196.

[135] David H. Bayley (1976): Forces of order: Police behaviour in Japan and the United States. Berkeley: University of California Press.

[136] Bayley (1976): Forces of order: Police behaviour in Japan and the United States: 17, 33.

[137] Ezra F. Vogel (1979): Japan as number one: Lessons for America. Cambridge: Harvard University Press: 204.

[138] Karel van Wolferen (1989): The Enigma of Japanese power: People and politics in a stateless nation. London: Macmillan: 183f.

[139] Peter J. Katzenstein and Yutaka Tsujinaka (1991): Defending the Japanese state: Structures, norms and the political responses to terrorism and violent social protest in the 1970s and 1980s. Ithaca: Cornell University East Asia Program: 35; Naoko Yoshida and Frank Leishman (2006): Japan. In: Trevor Jones and Tim Newburn (eds.): Plural policing: A comparative perspective. London: Routlegde. 222–238: 222; Walter L. Ames (1981): Police and community in Japan. Berkeley: University of California Press: 9f.

[140] Christopher Aldous (1997): The Police in Occupation Japan: Control, Corruption and Resistance to Reform. London: Routledge: 20.

[141] Frank Leishman (2007): Koban: Neighborhood Policing in Contemporary Japan. In: Policing, 1 (2), 196–202: 197; Ames (1981): Police and community in Japan: 23.

[142] Robin Ramcharan (2002): Forging a Singaporean statehood 1965–1995: The contribution of Japan. The Hague: Kluwer Law International: 235.

[143] Erika Fairchild and Harry R. Dammer (2001): Comparative criminal justice systems. Belmont: Wadsworth/Thomson Learning: 107; Ames (1981): Police and community in Japan: 38; Bayley (1976): Forces of order: Police behaviour in Japan and the United States: 84.

[144] Ramcharan (2002): Forging a Singaporean statehood 1965–1995; The contribution of Japan: 236.

[145] Katzenstein and Tsujinaka (1991): Defending the Japanese state: Structures, norms and the political responses to terrorism and violent social protest in the 1970s and 1980s: 44; van Wolferen (1989): The Enigma of Japanese power: People and politics in a stateless nation: 184.

[146] Fairchild and Dammer (2001): Comparative criminal justice systems: 109.

[147] Aldous (1997): The Police in Occupation Japan: Control, Corruption and Resistance to Reform: 36–38.

[148] Morio Onda (2013): Mutual help networks and social transformation in Japan. In: American Journal of Economics and Sociology, 72 (3), 531–564: 537.

[149] Peter J. Katzenstein and Yutaka Tsujinaka (2008): Japan's Internal Security Policy. In: Peter J. Katzenstein (ed.): Rethinking Japanese Security: Internal and External Dimensions. London: Routledge. 76–103: 85f.

[150] Katzenstein and Tsujinaka (1991): Defending the Japanese state: Structures, norms and the political responses to terrorism and violent social protest in the 1970s and 1980s: 93f; van Wolferen (1989): The Enigma of Japanese power: People and politics in a stateless nation: 185; Vogel (1979): Japan as number one: Lessons for America: 215.

[151] Aldous (1997): The Police in Occupation Japan: Control, Corruption and Resistance to Reform: 213.

[152] Katzenstein and Tsujinaka (1991): Defending the Japanese state: Structures, norms and the political responses to terrorism and violent social protest in the 1970s and 1980s: 54f; Ramcharan (2002): Forging a Singaporean statehood 1965–1995: The contribution of Japan: 237.

[153] Noriaki Kawamura and Yasuhiro Shirakawa (2008): Current Developments Affecting the Japanese Koban System Community Policing. In: Tom Williamson (ed.): The Handbook of Knowledge-Based Policing: Current Conceptions and Future Directions. Chichester: John Wiley & Sons. 157–174; Katzenstein and Tsujinaka (2008): Japan's Internal Security Policy: 85.

[154] Katzenstein and Tsujinaka (1991): Defending the Japanese state: Structures, norms and the political responses to terrorism and violent social protest in the 1970s and 1980s: 90.

[155] David Murakami Wood, David Lyon, and Kiyoshi Abe (2007): Surveillance in Urban Japan: A Critical Introduction. In: Urban Studies, 44 (3), 551–568: 554f.

[156] Rob I. Mawby (2003): Models of policing. In: Tim Newburn (ed.): Handbook of policing. Devon: Willan Publishing. 15–40: 33.

[157] Murakami Wood, Lyon, and Abe (2007): Surveillance in Urban Japan: A Critical Introduction: 555f; Katzenstein and Tsujinaka (1991): Defending the Japanese state: Structures, norms and the political responses to terrorism and violent social protest in the 1970s and 1980s: 91; van Wolferen (1989): The Enigma of Japanese power: People and politics in a stateless nation: 184f.

[158] Ames (1981): Police and community in Japan: 215.

[159] De La Rosa (2008): Aneignung oder Annäherung. Zwei Formen interkultureller Kommunikation: 86.

[160] Draude (2012): Die Vielfalt des Regierens: Eine Governance-Konzeption jenseits des Eurozentrismus: 236.

[161] Brogden (2005): "Horses for Courses" and "Thin Blue Lines": Community policing in transitional society: 65.

[162] See Graham Ellison (2007): Fostering a dependency culture: The commodification of community policing in a global marketplace. In: Andrew Goldsmith and James Sheptycki (eds.): Crafting transnational policing: Police capacity-building and global policing reform. Oxford: Hart Publishing. 203–242: 215; Brogden (2005): "Horses for Courses" and "Thin Blue Lines": Community policing in transitional society: 67; Steinberg (2011): Crime prevention goes abroad: Policy transfer and policing in post-apartheid South Africa: 350f; John Casey (2010): Policing world: The practice of international and transnational policing. Durham: Carolina Academic Press: 66–70; Ryan (2011): Statebuilding and Police Reform: The Freedom of Security: 130f.

[163] Mike Brogden (2004): Commentary: Community policing: A panacea from the West. In: African Affairs, 103 (413), 635–649: 638f; Ellison (2007): Fostering a dependency culture: The commodification of community policing in a global marketplace: 214.

[164] United Nations Security Council (2000): Report of the Secretary-General on the United Nations Transitional Administration in East Timor, S/2000/53, 26 January 2000. New York: United Nations. para. 51.

[165] Eirin Mobekk (2002): Policing from Below: Community Policing as an Objective in Peace Operations. In: Renata Dwan (ed.): Executive Policing: Enforcing the Law in Peace Operations. Oxford: Oxford University Press. 53–66: 53, 64.

[166] Bruce Baker (2008): Community policing in Freetown, Sierra Leone: Foreign import or local solution? In: Journal of Intervention and Statebuilding, 2 (1), 23–42: 23f.

[167] Kyed (2009): Community policing in post-war Mozambique: 357f; Brogden (2005): "Horses for Courses" and "Thin Blue Lines": Community policing in transitional society: 66f; Ellison (2007): Fostering a dependency culture: The commodification of community policing in a global marketplace: 213f; Organisation for Security and Co-operation in Europe (2008): Good practices in building police-public partnerships by the Senior Police Advisor to the OSCE Secretary General.

[168] Bruce Baker and Eric Scheye (2007): Multi-layered justice and security delivery in post-conflict and fragile states. In: Conflict, Security & Development, 7 (4), 503–528: 506–508; Ellison (2007): Fostering a dependency culture: The commodification of community policing in a global marketplace: 212.

[169] On the causal link between Singaporean community policing and the envisaged policing approach in Timor-Leste, see Mobekk (2002): Policing from Below: Community Policing as an Objective in Peace Operations: 53, 64.

[170] Scott Mainwaring (2015): Party system institutionalization: Reflections based on the Asian cases. In: Allen Hicken and Erik Martinez Kuhonta (eds.): Party system institutionalization in Asia: Democracies, autocracies, and the shadows of the past. Cambridge: Cambridge University Press. 328–348: 328ff; Netina Tan (2015): Institutionalized succession and hegemonic party cohesion in Singapore. In: Allen Hicken and Erik Martinez Kuhonta (eds.): Party system institutionalization in Asia: Democracies, autocracies, and the shadows of the past. Cambridge: Cambridge University Press. 49–73: 49–52.

[171] Ashraf Ghani and Claire Lockhart (2008): Fixing failed states; A framework for rebuilding a fractured world. Oxford: Oxford University Press: 35f.

[172] Jon S. T. Quah (1995): Crime prevention in a city state: The functions of the public police in Singapore. In: Koichi Miyazawa and Setsuo Miyazawa (eds.): Crime prevention in the urban community. Deventer: Kluwer Law International. 227–251: 232.

[173] Sinclair (2006): At the end of the line: Colonial policing and the imperial endgame 1945–80; Lindsay Clutterbuck (2015): The other side of COIN: New challenges for British police and military in the twenty-first century. In: Robert Johnson and Timothy Clack (eds.): At the end of military intervention: Historical, theoretical, and applied approaches to transition, handover, and withdrawal. Oxford: Oxford University Press. 437–456: 439f.

[174] Leng Leng Thang and S. K. Gan (2003): Deconstructing 'Japanisation': Reflections from the 'learn from Japan' campaign in Singapore. In: New Zealand Journal of Asian Studies, 5 (1), 91–106: 101; Quah (1995): Crime prevention in a city state: The functions of the public police in Singapore: 232.

[175] Vogel (1979): Japan as number one: Lessons for America.

[176] Ramcharan (2002): Forging a Singaporean statehood 1965-1995; The contribution of Japan: 228f.

[177] Bayley (1976): Forces of order: Police behaviour in Japan and the United States.

[178] See Christopher Aldous and Frank Leishman (1999): Police and community safety in Japan: Model or myth? In: Crime Prevention & Community Safety, 1 (1), 25–39: 27.

[179] Ramcharan (2002): Forging a Singaporean statehood 1965-1995: The contribution of Japan: 217.

[180] Quah (1995): Crime prevention in a city state: The functions of the public police in Singapore: 233; on the Singaporean security and defense policy see Tan Tai Yong (2011): The armed forces and politics in Singapore: The persistence of civil-military fusion. In: Marcus Mietzner (ed.): The political resurgence of the military in Southeast Asia: Conflict and leadership. London: Routledge. 148–166: 151.

181 Thang and Gan (2003): Deconstructing 'Japanisation': Reflections from the 'learn from Japan' campaign in Singapore: 102; Ramcharan (2002): Forging a Singaporean statehood 1965–1995: The contribution of Japan: 229.

182 Simon Avenell (2013): Beyond mimesis: Japan and the uses of political ideology in Singapore. In: Paul Morris, Naoko Shimazu, and Edward Vickers (eds.): Imagining Japan in post-war East Asia: Identity politics, schooling and popular culture. Abingdon: Routledge. 29–48: 41f; Quah (1995): Crime prevention in a city state: The functions of the public police in Singapore: 240f.

183 Avenell (2013): Beyond mimesis: Japan and the uses of political ideology in Singapore: 42; Ramcharan (2002): Forging a Singaporean statehood 1965–1995: The contribution of Japan: 228.

184 Thang and Gan (2003): Deconstructing 'Japanisation': Reflections from the 'learn from Japan' campaign in Singapore: 103; Quah (1995): Crime prevention in a city state: The functions of the public police in Singapore: 95.

185 Numerous campaigns on crime awareness as part of the community policing outreach, from the 1980s to present, can be found in: Susan Sim (2011): Making Singapore safe: Thirty years of the National Crime Prevention Council. Singapore: Marshall Cavendish Editions: 91–123.

186 Ramcharan (2002): Forging a Singaporean statehood 1965–1995; The contribution of Japan: 244.

187 Avenell (2013): Beyond mimesis: Japan and the uses of political ideology in Singapore: 44f; Pak Tee Ng and Hak Senk Ang (2011): Integrating quality and innovation: The case of the Singapore Police Force. In: Quality and Innovation, 1 (3), 237–251; Thang and Gan (2003): Deconstructing 'Japanisation': Reflections from the 'learn from Japan' campaign in Singapore: 103f.

188 Thang and Gan (2003): Deconstructing 'Japanisation': Reflections from the 'learn from Japan' campaign in Singapore: 102f.

189 Bethan K. Greener (2009): The new international policing. Basingstoke: Palgrave Macmillan; Ludovic Hood (2008): Missed opportunities: The United Nations, police service and defence force development in Timor-Leste, 1999–2004. In: Gordon Peake, Alice Hills, and Eric Scheye (eds.): Managing insecurity: Field experiences of security sector reform. New York: Routledge. 57–76; Kocak (2016): Security Sector Reconstruction in Post-Conflict: The Lessons from Timor-Leste.

190 On the Portuguese colonialism in Timor-Leste and its legacies, see Rod Nixon (2012): Justice and governance in East Timor: Indigenous approaches and the "New Subsistence State". London: Routledge; Monika Schlicher (1996): Portugal in Ost-Timor: Eine kritische Untersuchung zur portugiesischen Kolonialgeschichte in Ost-Timor 1850 bis 1912. Hamburg: Abera Verlag; Helio A. Esteves Felgas (1956): Timor Português. Lisbon: Agencia Geral do Ultramar; on the British colonialism in Southeast Asia, see Nicholas Tarling (2001): Imperialism in Southeast Asia, "A fleeting, passing phase". London: Routledge.

191 Mobekk (2002): Policing from Below: Community Policing as an Objective in Peace Operations: 53, 64.

192 United Nations Security Council (1999): Resolution 1272.

193 Kocak (2016): Security Sector Reconstruction in Post-Conflict: The Lessons from Timor-Leste: 350.

194 United Nations Security Council (2000): Report of the Secretary-General on the United Nations Transitional Administration in East Timor, S/2000/53.

195 Eirin Mobekk (2001): Policing Peace Operations: United Nations Civilian Police in East Timor. London: King's College: 8–10, 15; Michael G. Smith and Moreen Dee (2003): Peacekeeping in East Timor: The path to independence. Boulder: Lynne Rienner Publishers: 74f.

196 Interview with UNPOL officer, Dili, June 2011. Mobekk (2001): Policing Peace Operations: United Nations Civilian Police in East Timor: 12f.

[197] Schroeder, Chappuis, and Kocak (2014): Security Sector Reform and the Emergence of Hybrid Security Governance: 224.

[198] Japan International Cooperation Agency (2008): JICA Timor-Leste Annual Report 2007. Dili: JICA Timor-Leste Office: 20.

[199] Interview with JICA official, Dili, August 2012.

[200] United Nations Mission of Support in East Timor (UNMISET) followed UNMIT. UNMISET was active in Timor-Leste from 2002 until 2005.

[201] Sue Emmott, Manuhuia Barcham, Taimoor Ali Khan, and Eduardo Soares (2010): Community policing pilot programme Timor-Leste: Independent review report, 18. April 2010. Wellington: NZAID; Bevan and MacKenzie (2012): 'Cowboy' Policing versus 'the Softer Stuff': 508.

[202] Interview with international SSR advisor, Dili, August 2012.

[203] Democratic Republic of Timor-Leste (2009): Decree-Law No. 9/2009. The Organic Law of Timor-Leste's National Police (PNTL). Dili: Democratic Republic of Timor-Leste.

[204] Interview with director of local NGO, Dili, August 2012. See also International Crisis Group (2010): Timor-Leste: Time for the UN to step back, Asia Briefing No. 116. Brussels: ICG. 3; International Crisis Group (2013): Timor-Leste: Stability at what cost?, Asia Report No. 246. Brussels: ICG. 23.

[205] Interview with UNPOL officer, Dili, August 2012. See also Nélson De Sousa C. Belo and Mark R. Koenig (2011): Institutionalizing community policing in Timor-Leste: Exploring the politics of police reform, Occasional Paper 9. Dili: The Asia Foundation.

[206] On the issue of the F-FDTL's role expansion, see Deniz Kocak (2014): Timor-Leste: The continuing challenge of police building and security governance. In: Security Sector Reform Resource Centre, http://www.ssrresourcecentre.org/2014/08/19/timor-leste-the-continuing-challenge-of-police-building-and-security-governance/ [accessed on 22 August 2014].

[207] Interview with UN official, Dili, August 2012. See also Henri Myrttinen (2014): Do as we say, not as we do? Gender and police reform in Timor-Leste. In: Felix Heiduk (ed.): Security sector reform in Southeast Asia: From policy to practice. Basingstoke: Palgrave. 181–200: 190f.

[208] Interview with PNTL officer, Dili, August 2012.

[209] Fundasaun Mahein (2011): Development in the National Police of Timor-Leste, Mahein Nia Lian No. 21, 21. July 2011. Dili: Fundasaun Mahein. 23.

[210] Interview with PNTL officer, Dili, August 2012; see also Schroeder, Chappuis, and Kocak (2014): Security Sector Reform and the Emergence of Hybrid Security Governance: 225f.

[211] International Crisis Group (2009): Handing back responsibility to Timor-Leste's Police. Asia Report No. 180. Brussels: ICG. 23.

[212] Interview with TLPDP officer, Dili, July 2011.

[213] Interview with TLPDP officer, Dili, August 2012.

[214] Interview with international policy advisor, Dili, August 2012.

[215] Polisia Nasional de Timor Leste (2012): "Mata-Dalan" Treinamentu materia polisiamentu komunitaria Timor Leste. Dili: Polisia Nasional de Timor Leste.

[216] Interview with international policy advisor, Dili, August 2012.

[217] Interview with international police advisers, Dili, December 2015; Fundasaun Mahein (2015): Implementation Policy of the Community Policing in Timor-Leste, Mahein's Thought No. 8, 30. July 2015. Dili: Fundasaun Mahein: 24; Todd Wassel (2016): Reforming Security in Timor-Leste: Can a Plural Justice System Work? Dili: Asia Foundation.

[218] Interview with international police advisers, Dili, December 2015; Fundasaun Mahein (2015): Implementasaun VIP iha instituisaun PNTL "Prespetiva Sosiedade Sivil". Dili: Fundasaun Mahein.

[219] Polisia Nasional de Timor Leste (2013): PNTL Strategic Plan 2014–2018. Dili: PNTL General Command / Department of Administration and Planning.

220 On the Indonesian occupation of Timor-Leste, see John G. Taylor (1999): East Timor: The price of freedom. London: Zed Books; Carmel Budiardjo and Liem Soei Liong (1984): The War Against East Timor. London: Zed Books.

221 See the part on the Japanese *tonari-gumi* in chapter 3 of this paper.

222 Leonard C. Sebastian (2006): Realpolitik Ideology: Indonesia's Use of Military Forces. Singapore: ISEAS: 277f; on the overall Japanese impact on the military in Indonesia, see Joyce C. Lebra (2010): Japanese-Trained Armies in Southeast Asia. Singapore: ISEAS.

223 Sebastian (2006): Realpolitik Ideology: Indonesia's Use of Military Forces: 278.

224 Damien Kingsbury (2003): Power Politics and the Indonesian Military. London: RoutledgeCurzon: 31; Deniz Kocak (2015): Beyond Control: Militias as Inherent Part of the National Security Policy in Indonesia. In: Sicherheit und Frieden / Security and Peace, 33 (4), 212–217: 213.

225 Peter Bartu (2000): The militia, the military, and the people of Bobonaro district. In: Bulletin of Concerned Asian Scholars, 32 (1), 35–42: 36; FUNU (1989): A administração indonesia em Timor-Leste, 17–20. 19; Sebastian (2006): Realpolitik Ideology: Indonesia's Use of Military Forces: 139, 289.

226 Todd Wassel (2014): Institutionalising community policing in Timor-Leste: Police development in Asia's youngest country, ODI Report. London: Overseas Development Institute. 17.

227 Interview with PNTL officer, Dili, October 2015.

228 Interview with PNTL officer, Bobonaro District, November 2015.

229 Interview with director of local NGO, Dili, November 2015; Wassel (2016): Reforming Security in Timor-Leste: Can a Plural Justice System Work?

230 Interviews with PNTL officers, Bobonaro and Baucau district, November 2015.

231 Interview with PNTL officer, Baucau district, November 2015; see also Fundasaun Mahein (2015): Implementation Policy of the Community Policing in Timor-Leste, Mahein's Thought No. 8, 30. July 2015: 22.

232 Interviews with local NGO chairmen, Dili, October 2015.

233 Interview with director of local NGO, Dili, November 2015; interviews with PNTL officers, Dili, November 2015.

234 Interview with international police advisers, Dili, December 2015.

235 Belo and Koenig (2011): Institutionalizing community policing in Timor-Leste: Exploring the politics of police reform, Occasional Paper 9. Dili: The Asia Foundation. 19.

236 Eirin Mobekk (2005): Identifying lessons in United Nations international policing missions, Policy Paper No 9. Geneva: Geneva Centre for the Democratic Control of Armed Forces (DCAF); Hood (2008): Missed opportunities: The United Nations, police service and defence force development in Timor-Leste, 1999–2004; Kocak (2016): Security Sector Reconstruction in Post-Conflict: The Lessons from Timor-Leste.

237 Interview with international police adviser, Dili, August 2012; Myrttinen (2014): Do as we say, not as we do? Gender and police reform in Timor-Leste; Schroeder, Chappuis, and Kocak (2014): Security Sector Reform and the Emergence of Hybrid Security Governance: 224.

238 Belo and Koenig (2011): Institutionalizing community policing in Timor-Leste: Exploring the politics of police reform, Occasional Paper 9. Dili: The Asia Foundation; Kocak (2016): Security Sector Reconstruction in Post-Conflict: The Lessons from Timor-Leste.

239 See, among others, Fundasaun Mahein (2011): PNTL's weapons: Items of security or intimidation?, Mahein Nia Lian No. 25, 30. November 2011. Dili: Fundasaun Mahein; Fundasaun Mahein (2011): Saida Mak Operasaun Ualu-Ualu (88)? In: Fundasaun Mahein, https://fundasaunmahein.wordpress.com/2011/08/10/saida-mak-operasaun-ualu-ualu-88/ [Accessed on 13 February 2012]; Human Rights Watch (2006): Tortured beginnings: Police violence and the beginnings of impunity in East Timor, Human Rights Watch 18 (2). New York: Human

Rights Watch; International Crisis Group (2008): Timor-Leste: Security Sector Reform, Asia Report No. 143. Brussels: ICG.

[240] On the British legacy of policing and bureaucratic capacity building in Singapore, see Sinclair (2006): At the end of the line: Colonial policing and the imperial endgame 1945–80; and Clutterbuck (2015): The other side of COIN: New challenges for British police and military in the twenty-first century: 439f; Jon S. T. Quah (2003): Public administration in Singapore: The role of the public bureaucracy in a one-party dominant system. In: Krishna K. Tummala (ed.): Comparative bureaucratic systems. Lanham: Lexington Books. 165–183.

[241] See Draude (2012): Die Vielfalt des Regierens: Eine Governance-Konzeption jenseits des Eurozentrismus: 244; but also De La Rosa (2008): Aneignung oder Annäherung. Zwei Formen interkultureller Kommunikation; and Paulmann (1998): Interkultureller Transfer zwischen Deutschland und Großbritannien: Einführung in ein Forschungskonzept.

[242] Bayley and Perito (2010): The Police in War: Fighting Insurgency, Terrorism, and Violent Crime. 3.

[243] Christopher Murphy (2007): The cart before the horse: Community oriented versus professional models of international police reform. In: Andrew Goldsmith and James Sheptycki (eds.): Crafting transnational policing: Police capacity-building and global policing reform. Oxford: Hart Publishing. 243–262; Brogden (2005): "Horses for Courses" and "Thin Blue Lines": Community policing in transitional society; Nicolas Lemay-Hébert (2009): UNPOL and police reform in Timor-Leste: Accomplishments and setbacks. In: International Peacekeeping, 16 (3), 393–406; Mobekk (2005): Identifying lessons in United Nations international policing missions, Policy Paper No 9. Geneva: Geneva Centre for the Democratic Control of Armed Forces (DCAF).

www.ingramcontent.com/pod-product-compliance
Lightning Source LLC
Chambersburg PA
CBHW081651270326
41933CB00018B/3426